EARTHQUAKE IN THE CITY

'My children, the alarm bells are sounding all over Europe, for judgement is being spoken out over the nations. Over your nation, Great Britain, a mighty earthquake is about to occur, an earthquake that will swallow up the whole City. Whole companies and city institutions will collapse in this earthquake, some never to rise again.

'My judgement that has been withheld for so long must now be unleashed on your nation in order that my church repent and lead this nation in repentance, for I am a righteous and holy God, just in all my ways, a God who longs to show mercy, but one who will no longer tolerate the unrighteousness of my dear church. It is out of love that I visit this nation with judgement – you must know that this must always be the case. My children, repent now before it is too late, for already the day of my return draws near and you must not be found wanting, like the virgins who did not fill their lamps with oil; but awake, my children, and be my watchmen, and speak with a prophetic voice of the judgement that is about to come upon the nations.

'If you repent and turn from your wicked ways, I will visit your nation, Great Britain, once again, not with judgement, but with revival power, and I will protect you from all the strategy of the enemy.

'In regard to Europe, come out of her, my dear children, for she will align herself with the Beast and the False Prophet who will arise and appear for just a short while. My children, take heart, for I am with you always. Do not give up, but pray without ceasing and see the salvation of your God.'

The prophecy given to Paul Slennett in February 1989

Earthquake in the City

Clifford Denton and Paul Slennett

KINGSWAY PUBLICATIONS
EASTBOURNE

First published 1997

ISBN 0 85476 639 1

Designed and produced by Bookprint Creative Services
P.O. Box 827, BN21 3YJ, England for
KINGSWAY PUBLICATIONS LTD
Lottbridge Drove, Eastbourne, East Sussex BN23 6NT.
Printed in Great Britain.

This book is dedicated to our parents,
Sydney and Evelyn Denton and
Florence Slennett,
in appreciation of the foundations that were
placed in our lives through them and others
of their generation.

Contents

Acknowledgements

The authors of this book would like to acknowledge the lives and ministries of those who have gone before us, those who have contended for the true Christian faith in Britain over many centuries, many of whom were martyrs. We acknowledge, in a special way, those in the present generation who pray for this nation, and others who have written and spoken on issues related to this book, helping us to form the background to our own interpretation of the prophecy which we are proclaiming.

There are those who have influenced our own Christian growth and been patient with us through years of gaining the experience in ministry necessary for a work such as this. Some will find echoes of their teaching and influence in the chapters of this book, and we trust they will be pleased to share in its fruitfulness for the kingdom.

We would also like to acknowledge the help and support of close friends and colleagues who have encouraged us and helped with research, corrections, typing, proofreading and the overall development of the book. We would like to thank the publishers for their partnership of faith in the production of this book, and our families for their patience and support close to home.

We are ultimately indebted to Almighty God for not treating us as our sins deserve and for inspiring us to sound the trumpet to bring a warning and a clear call to repentance.

The Coronation Oath

The Archbishop or bishop shall say:

Will you solemnely promise and sweare to governe the people of this kingdome of England and the dominions thereto belonging according to the statutes in Parlyament agreed on and the laws and customs of the same?

The King and Queene shall say,

I solemnly promise soe to doe.

Archbishop or bishop:

Will you to your power cause law and justice in mercy to be executed in all your judgements?

King and Queene:

I will.

Archbishop or bishop:

Will you to the utmost of your power maintaine the laws of God the true profession of the Gospell and the Protestant reformed religion established by law? And will you preserve unto the bishops and clergy of this realme and to the churches committed to their charge all such rights and privileges as by law doe or shall appertaine unto them or any of them?

King and Queene:

All this I promise to doe.

After this the King and Queene laying his and her hand upon the Holy Gospells shall say

King and Queene:

The things which I have here before promised I will performe and keepe
Soe help me God.

Then the King and Queene shall kisse the booke.

Introduction

Does God speak today? We believe that he does, and that he has sent a warning to Great Britain. The warning is about economic troubles ahead, which will come suddenly and have far-reaching consequences. This is a judgement from God because of the way the nation has drifted away from him.

God will not necessarily speak to us in ways we expect. We might not even realise that he is speaking at all. When he does speak, it is because of his great love for us, for we are a part of his own creation. It is because of his mercy that he communicates with us, because he wants us to live in trust and fellowship with him.

Britain has a history of belief in God and has had access to the Bible for more than a thousand years. The Bible teaches us the way to live in accordance with God's plan for mankind. In its pages we see a reflection of our individual lives and we can learn about God's ways. He has been active through all history and he continues to communicate with every generation. The Bible tells us that God exists and that he speaks in different ways: through the natural world, in our individual lives, in the workings of society, through the Bible itself, and through the prophetic word for today.

God walks and talks daily with those who earnestly seek him, bringing blessings and encouragement along the path of life. Even when we go away from him he continues to send warnings, in whatever way he chooses. There is ample evidence for this in the history of Britain. He has protected us and delivered us many times, and we have honoured him through our laws and through the way we have established our society. Britain has been a base from which Christian missionaries have gone out into the world to bear witness to the truth of the living God of the Bible and to salvation through his Son Jesus Christ.

Britain has not been invaded for nearly one thousand years, and has known miraculous deliverances from the Spanish Armada and during the two World Wars. During the Second World War this was openly acknowledged by the King and Prime Minister at such crucial times as the evacuation from Dunkirk and during the Battle of Britain. God has been with us during many times of need, as we have called upon him from the heart.

In recent years, however, we have seen a growing opposition to biblical principles. The love of money has replaced the love of God at the heart of the nation. We have moved into a time of relative morality, into permissiveness of every kind, and we are reaping the consequences in disharmony and discontent. Where are our absolute standards? Where is our protection now?

We believe that God has sent a warning to Britain. It is an important warning which we believe must be given to the whole nation. The Bible tells us that we reap what we sow (Galatians 6:7). If we sow righteousness, that is what we shall reap, in terms of God's protection and safe-keeping, even if we don't fully understand how he helps us. If we sow unrighteousness, we will eventually reap disaster, as God's protection is removed.

In the New Testament Book of Hebrews we read, 'It is a dreadful thing to fall into the hands of the living God' (Hebrews 10:31). This was written about people who deliberately reject salvation through Jesus Christ, the Son of God, who shed his blood for them. It is a warning of the judgement which comes upon the enemies of God. The warning is directed at those who once knew the truth but have now rejected it. There is no way to find peace with God when the only offer of peace is rejected. There is no other sacrifice for sins for those who reject the sacrifice of God's only Son, Jesus Christ.

This message from the Book of Hebrews could have been written for the people of Great Britain in our day. We are a nation which has been at the front line of God's purposes and has known his blessings. We have known godliness through our legal system, through our education system and through our institutions, including the monarchy, the church and the government. The British Empire was the largest empire that the world has known. Surely God gave us this empire in order to serve the world. There have been times when Great Britain has been truly great, but out of service and not pride. We have gone further than most nations to develop a governmental system which can be led by the guiding hand of God. It has never been a perfect nation but it has been a bright light in a dark world and God has chosen to use the nation for his purposes and to bless us. But now the nation is in decline and this coincides with a general turning away from God.

This book tells of a prophetic warning to our nation. By this we mean that God has spoken in a certain way to us, and has given us the task of declaring and explaining what he has said. Prophecy is God's way of communicating to people in this world and prophets are his mouthpiece, raised up for a certain time and purpose. The proclamations of God's messages to mankind go out week after week from the pulpits of churches, as preachers interpret the Bible's teaching for today's society. In addition, God will speak in other clear ways when it is appropriate. True prophecy can always be tested against the teaching of the Bible.

When God speaks in this way, it is not too late for the nation to turn to God. There may come a time when the nation is no longer able to recognise the voice of God. Then spiritual darkness and deception will follow and people will reap the harvest of their own evil ways. We may not have reached this time in our nation – but it could come. When it does, however, no one will be able to say that warnings were not given and the way back to God's blessings clearly offered.

It is an awesome responsibility to warn a whole nation, but that is what this book is about. The responsibility is to give the warning clearly and with right understanding. The warning does not come from a God who delights in people suffering, but from the God and Father of the Lord Jesus Christ, who is a holy God whose righteous acts are the result of perfect love and justice. He is a God who has the right to abandon us but who withholds judgement to give us time to hear his words and turn to him. Even as the most horrific sins are committed in our nation he holds out his promises of blessings, if only we will turn to him, repent and be reconciled and healed. No sin takes us beyond God's forgiveness, if we truly repent and accept the sacrifice of his Son and his lordship in our lives. He desires that we are thoroughly rebuilt as a nation and he will send warning after warning.

Yet if warnings are constantly rejected there will come a time when judgement is inevitable and decline is certain. God cannot keep on protecting a nation that constantly wars against him.

This book could have been a straightforward prophetic warning with no explanation, but the love of God urges us also to give explanations of why he is sending warnings and what he expects us to do. We see hope as well as urgency. It is not too late for the older generations of our nation to remember the height from which we have fallen and to lead the nation back to godly ways before a younger generation takes over, many of whom have not been properly schooled in the ways of God. Otherwise it will become the blind leading the blind. It is our hope that we will quicken something in the minds and hearts and memories of many of our readers, which will persuade them of the rightness of this warning. We want to gain the confidence of those who are willing to take action before it is too late. God is calling to us as a father calls to a child whom he loves, but who is in danger.

The prophecy itself concerns a mighty earthquake which will affect the financial institutions of our nation. This understanding has come as we have prayed together for several years, and considered how to deliver the prophecy. We anticipate that there will be a sudden disturbance of the economy, destabilising it at its foundations, which will have far-reaching effects, both financial and social. The financial earthquake, we believe, is to be accompanied by a sudden and surprising physical earthquake which, like the hurricane that accompanied the financial problems of 1987, will be a sign from God and a part of his overall judgement.

We trust that the publishing of the book will be timed to make the maximum impact with its message. Rationally speaking one might suppose that anyone could prophesy economic decline when it has already begun, but it is our view that the decline has not reached the bottom yet and that, when it does, the signs of God's judgement will be evident in a dramatic way, perhaps at a time when there is growing confidence in financial recovery. This will be the first of perhaps three major warnings, but woe to our nation if we do not heed the first of these warnings!

A woe is the opposite of a blessing. When we are blessed we have a sense of protection and well-being. A woe comes as a result of protection being removed. We become vulnerable and fear the consequences of the troubles that come into our lives.

We have tried to write this book in a positive style, declaring the certainty of what we believe. Who bothers to respond to a trumpet that does not have a clear sound? This will be welcomed by those ready to respond to a clear warning but it may infuriate those who will not respond. Our book is addressed to both groups. The former can find a way to personal relationship with a loving heavenly Father. The latter will walk into judgement of their own free will and have no excuse. We desire that the former group is maximised and the latter group minimised.

The judgement on our nation will be through economic collapse of such proportions that it will be like an earthquake in the City. The relationship between the financial earthquake and its physical counterpart remains to be seen, but we have no doubt that, taken together, they will amount to a mighty woe. This will be the first of three possible woes to come to the nation. The second two are conditional and the nation needs simply to respond to the first woe. Indeed, we have not been told what the following two woes will be. We have been urged to pray that we will not have to find out. The full text of the prophecy is given on page 1, and in Chapters 3 and 6 of this book.

How can a nation respond and be drawn back into God's protection? The answer lies partly in what Britain has achieved in the past: in godly laws, in education systems that teach about God and his ways, in family life that honours God, in having the Bible as the nation's open book affecting every aspect of the life of the nation, instead of a closed book gathering dust on our bookshelves. A nation cannot be saved as a whole for the afterlife; salvation comes only to individuals who respond to Jesus Christ for themselves. But a nation can establish a framework which God can bless, and in which individuals can hear about God and his works and ways and come to salvation through Jesus Christ.

We have arranged the book so that the prophecy can be read with understanding. Our aim is to give sufficient biblical teaching to demonstrate how prophetic warnings are part of God's ways. It is of the utmost importance that we not only understand prophecy but also that we understand God. The book is addressed to all the people of Britain, to the learned and the unschooled, to the leaders and to all the people, whether rich or poor, to those in the church and to those outside it.

Paul Slennett was inspired some years ago to promote a proclamation that *Jesus is alive!* This message was carried as a Royal Mail postmark throughout Britain and also into almost every country of the world around Easter 1988. This was a statement of truth, an invitation to consider and respond to this great truth and a prophetic warning. Because Jesus is alive it is necessary for everyone to turn to him, give their lives to him who died for their sins, and trust in him. The simple message should have been a reminder to the nation and could have been a prompt to joyful worship across the nation. It was one of many evangelistic projects to take place across Britain in recent years.

The message of John 3:16 is a well-known and wonderful message of salvation through Jesus:

> For God so loved the world that he gave his one and only Son, that whoever believes in him shall not perish but have eternal life.

But only a few verses later in the same chapter we read:

> Whoever believes in him is not condemned, but whoever does not believe stands condemned already because he has not believed in the name of God's one and only Son. This is the verdict: light has come into the world, but men loved darkness instead of light because their deeds were evil.

Those who reject the message that Jesus is alive to give them salvation simply walk into a world which is judged already, on account of not accepting the Son.

So the same message can be read as a message of salvation or of judgement. Indeed, the One who came to save will return as the Judge of all and we will be judged on the basis of whether we believed in the One who died and rose again and is alive today.

We thought it appropriate, therefore, to include a chapter which shows the development of the *Jesus is Alive!* postmark. This is a testimony to a faithful God. He is indeed alive and loves his fallen creation enough to keep telling them.

We go on to draw lessons from the prophets of the Bible, showing how their messages are also relevant to Britain today. They had messages for the nation of Israel, and it is right that we study these as we consider the woes and blessings of our nation.

We explore the decline in godliness in our nation, and we have a strong word for the church. It is one thing to tell a godless nation about God's laws and righteous judgements. It is another to address the decay in the church where God's principles should be held firm and taught to the nation. The church will not escape the judgements of God if it has failed to do this. Indeed there is a sense in which it is held accountable for the decline of the nation: 'It is time for judgement to begin with the family of God' (1 Peter 4:17).

Having explored this background to prophecy and righteous judgement, the way is clear for an understanding of the judgement which is about to fall on Britain through her economy. This is a direct judgement on a major source of corruption in Britain today, showing mankind that there is no strength in human systems without God. This word has been pronounced from heaven and there is no man mighty enough to withstand its effects. It can be a miracle of God's provision because when the power of finance is removed the nation should be ready to fall to its knees. This judgement can be redemptive, meaning that it is a shock from a loving God who wants us to turn to him, and everyone should feel the clear call to turn to God and will have all the necessary indications that this is the work of God.

We will explore the potential consequences of an economic collapse. There are likely to be immense repercussions, far more serious at all levels of society than we have yet seen. Our message, however, is for men and women to seek God for the rebuilding of the nation. He will expect a turning from ungodliness and a regeneration of laws which reflect his teaching. Such laws can cause him to protect this nation once more, but he will also expect our institutions to turn away from greed and unrighteousness. He will expect us to return to godly ways in the nurture of our children and the order of our families. It is not difficult to analyse the decay in our society which has accompanied the decline in our nation's laws and ideals, and this we will do.

The rise of Europe as a confederation of nations is related to this judgement on Britain. We include a chapter which refers to the warnings in the prophecy that we must come out of this alliance. The alliance is not based on a desire for godliness and is leading the nations of Europe into danger. If Britain is drifting from God now, how much more will this become the case when she is part of a larger humanistic empire. The weakness of such empires is seen when comparisons are made with the seemingly mighty empires of history: mighty in the eyes of man, but now fallen by the hand of God.

The glorious gospel of the kingdom must be the climax of this book. The ultimate objective of God, even though he will send earthquakes to warn us, is that we become members of the kingdom of heaven. This is the true theme and the purpose of this book. We trust that many will see the economic earthquake and its physical counterpart as a true warning from a loving God, and that there will be a ready response to the invitation to repent and be saved and secure. Even if the nation does not repent as a whole, any individual may do so, and thus begin to grow in a secure relationship with our heavenly Father. The riches of his kingdom do not depend on personal finance or success in business. These are dross in comparison with salvation through God's one and only Son Jesus Christ. God will demonstrate this by taking away our financial gods.

Our prayer is that this will be the only book that we have to write about the woeful judgement coming on this nation.

'Blessed is the nation whose God is the Lord' (Psalm 33:12).

1
1988 – A Year to Look Back

> Stand at the crossroads and look; ask for the ancient paths, ask where the good way is, and walk in it, and you will find rest for your souls (Jeremiah 6:16).

God is the God of history. In the Bible one nation, the nation of Israel, was chosen by God to be taught his ways. Their history is one of ordinary human beings being led by Almighty God. God showed them his blessings, his deliverance and his miracles. But what he taught Israel was not for them alone; it was for the whole world. The climax of history came when the full revelation of God the Father was demonstrated through Jesus Christ his only Son, who offered himself as a sacrifice for the sins of the world, and was raised from the dead to be seated at the right hand of the Father. Before he went to be with the Father he opened the way for the gospel message to be preached to the whole world. Now, nearly two thousand years later, millions of people have accepted God's plan of salvation, and, through the Bible account, have learned about the ways of God. They have come to faith in Jesus Christ. The fact that Jesus is alive is the climax of the Bible account and the foundation upon which all of our trust in God rests. The proclamation that *Jesus is alive!* is a statement which has influenced people from every generation for nearly two thousand years. It has transformed the lives of individuals, families and communities. It has brought order and blessing to nations.

Christianity comes to Britain

As far as we can tell, the message came to Great Britain very soon after the first apostles went out from Jerusalem in the first century AD. Britain has been a nation which has accepted the truth of the gospel message and has known the guiding hand of God. Much of Britain's history is a direct result of our acceptance of biblical truth. We are not written into the pages of the Bible as the nation of Israel is, but God has been guiding and helping us, and our history reminds us of his faithfulness.

We, in Britain, have been privileged to lead the world in honouring the Bible and seeking to serve the God of the Bible. We made it our aim that all men and women should have an understanding of the Scriptures and access to them. When the Bible was not in written form its truths were put into song, as far back as AD 664, when the Anglo-Saxon cowherd, Caedman of Whitby, applied his poetic gifts to recounting Bible stories from Creation to the Last Judgement. Bede, who lived from AD 674 to 753, and who was thought to be the most learned scholar in Western Europe, wrote many books relating the truths of the Bible and he translated the Gospel of John into Anglo-Saxon.

King Alfred, who reigned from AD 871 to 899 is thought by many to be the greatest of all English kings. England had been united under King Egbert in the early part of the ninth century, only to come under threat of invading Danes. Having checked this invasion, King Alfred then put aside every other personal ambition to dedicate his life to serving the nation. The laws of Britain were codified. The Ten Commandments were prefixed to these laws, as were other sections from the laws of Moses. Alfred is also viewed as the father of English literature, thus laying a foundation for the Bible to be translated later into English.

It was in 1538 that, by an Act of Parliament, copies of the Great Bible were placed in every church for anyone to read. This was possible on account of the work of William Tyndale who translated the Bible into English. Previously only the Latin translation was available and this only to the wealthy and to the clergy. The invention of the printing press made this possible, along with the work of men like Tyndale who devoted themselves to this task, even at the cost of their lives (Tyndale was executed in 1536 for his work of translation). Thereafter, the Bible was at the centre of Britain's society and government. All could learn from it and it was used in the framing of laws and the teaching of our children.

The Reformation

Up to the Reformation, Europe was dominated by the Roman Catholic system. The government of the Popes from Rome had become corrupt and ordinary people were in bondage to a religious system which did not represent the true gospel message. The Protestant

Reformers brought about a freedom of worship and a move across Europe whereby Christianity could grow without the bondage of Roman rule. This was a costly enterprise. Just as Tyndale lost his life to bring us the Bible in English, so many of the Reformers became martyrs so that others might be free.

Britain was greatly influenced by the Protestant Reformation, so much so that it eventually established a system whereby the monarchy vowed before God not to let Roman Catholic rule take Britain captive again, and also to uphold the teaching of the Protestant faith.

In 1588, 150 ships set off from Spain to remove Elizabeth I from the English throne and put the Catholic Mary Queen of Scots in her place. England had a fleet of no more than thirty-five ships, yet God clearly intervened on our behalf. There is an inscription at Plymouth Hoe commemorating this which says, 'God blew with His winds and they were scattered.'

The Spanish fleet attempted to escape north from the English fire ships in the English Channel. They went around the north of Scotland and then southwards past the west coast of Ireland but, along the way, ships were wrecked by furious storms which crippled and sank much of the fleet, while not one English fighting ship was lost. This defeat of the Spanish Armada ensured that rule of the seas passed to Britain, the Protestant Reformation was secured, and Britain was able to develop her Christian heritage.

Like England, Scotland became a stronghold of the true Christian faith after a stand was taken against Roman rule. The National Covenant was signed by 3,250 people in 1638 in Scotland. Some of the signatures were in blood, and the rise of the Covenanters was at the expense of many martyrs. Through this Covenant, the leaders of the Protestant Church in Scotland stood against the power of Rome which had overshadowed Scotland. The Reformed faith, as given in the 1580 Confession of Faith, was established.

Again, in England, there came about a confrontation which led to what has been called the Glorious Revolution. It followed the trial of seven bishops at Westminster Hall. This provided the focal point for a showdown between the divine right of kings, and parliamentary and individual freedoms. The miracle of the Glorious Revolution was achieved totally without bloodshed. The Accession of William and Mary followed and the monarchy of Britain became Protestant. Acts of Parliament, including the Bill of Rights, consolidated the religious and political liberties secured by the Revolution. These freedoms are now taken for granted but we must understand that the immense blessings we have experienced, even up to the present day, are linked to the rise of a law system and governmental system based on the teaching of the Bible.

The Coronation Oath

In 1688, with the passing of the Coronation Oath Act, Britain made an ongoing covenant with God. Such a covenant has had immense repercussions for the nation. It was an attempt to bind the government, the church and the monarchy together into a framework which God could bless. Indeed, it was a framework into which God was expected to speak and apply his own sovereign rule. The Bible was accepted as the guide for all our affairs and we framed an agreement which God can bless if we continue to honour what we have declared. At every coronation, the Archbishop of the Church of England asks the incoming monarch: 'Will you to the utmost of your power maintain the laws of God, the true profession of the gospel and the Protestant reformed religion established by law? And will you preserve unto the bishops and clergy of this realm and to the churches committed to their charge all such rights and privileges as by law do or shall appertain unto them or any of them?'

The King and Queen then answers: 'All this I promise to do.'

Then laying their hands upon the Bible they say: 'The things which I have here before promised I will perform and keep, so help me God.'

They then kiss the Bible.

It is also customary for two leading churchmen to present the monarch with the Bible, referring to it as 'the most valuable thing that this world affords', and also saying, 'Here is wisdom; this is the royal law; these are the lively oracles of God.' In accordance with tradition, these statements were included in the coronation of Queen Elizabeth II.

This indicates the extent to which we have gone in Britain to live in ways which please God. History books show, more fully than we can write here, how this nation has been recognised by the world as being blessed and used by God. Here, surely, is one reason at least for our nation's prosperity and peace.

Great men of God

John and Charles Wesley came at a time when Britain was in desperate need of hearing the gospel message afresh. They and a small group of others, including George Whitefield, met together while at Oxford University to pray and to live their lives methodically according to the New Testament. In 1735 John Wesley accepted an invitation to go to America. It is recorded that he said of this, 'I went to America to convert the Indians, but, oh, who shall convert me?' When back in England he experienced what was to be true conversion to the Christian faith, rather than simply a religious Christian lifestyle. On Wednesday, 24th May 1738, John went to a society in Aldersgate Street where Luther's preface to the Epistle to the Romans was being read. During this reading John experienced his conversion as the Holy Spirit of God came upon him. He put it this way:

> About a quarter before nine while he was describing the change which God works in the heart through faith in Christ, I felt my heart strangely warmed. I felt I did trust in Christ, in Christ alone for salvation and an assurance was given me, that he had taken away my sins, even mine, and saved me from the law of sin and death.

John Wesley and George Whitefield became powerful preachers who led thousands to faith in Jesus Christ in Britain, as they preached to crowds up and down the land. They were preachers and social reformers. The hymns of Charles Wesley were also agents of this revival, and such was the impact of Christianity in Britain that the world would come to consider us to be a Christian nation. Our whole law structure was turned towards the laws of God, and social improvements and reforms followed in the wake.

John Bunyan touched many lives through his

writing and his understanding of true Christianity. His *Pilgrim's Progress* has been an inspiration to every generation since he wrote it.

We sent out men like David Livingstone, who not only resisted slavery in Africa but opened the way for trade, for the dignity of the African people and for the gospel message. Men like William Carey were pioneers of mission too, opening the world to the Christian gospel. Such men were ordinary in the world's eyes, but raised up by God to do extraordinary things in the world. William Carey was a cobbler who caught a vision for world mission, went to India, and was recognised as a social reformer as well as a linguist and preacher. He was self-taught in the languages of India and, through his dedication, he enabled millions to read the Bible in their own language. He learned to live by faith for God's provision of all his needs, and was inspired to use the phrase, 'Expect great things from God. Attempt great things for God.'

These men stand as examples of the many pioneers who have moved the world with the transforming reality of the gospel message, making Britain unique in her stand for truth and righteousness, and even in her government systems.

A special year

The year 1988 was a very significant one for looking back over the history of Christianity in Britain, so that we might consider how God has blessed us, helped us and used us for his purposes. Here are a few of the significant milestones, already highlighted in this chapter, which show how Christianity was accepted at the heart of Britain, how the Bible was made available and how Christians, from this country, served the world and served God. In 1988 it was:

450 years since the Bible in English became available in every English parish.
400 years since the Bible was translated into Welsh.
400 years since the Spanish Armada was defeated.
350 years since the signing of the National Covenant in Scotland.
300 years since the 'Glorious Revolution'.
300 years since the Bill of Rights.
300 years since the death of John Bunyan.
300 years since the Coronation Oath Act.
250 years since the conversion of John and Charles Wesley.
200 years since the death of Charles Wesley.
200 years since William Carey began to consider seriously the problem of world mission.
150 years since David Livingstone was accepted as a candidate of the London Missionary Society.
150 years since the abolition of slavery in the British Empire.

Among the anniversaries that have been listed there are some of the most significant in British history. Surely God intended us to notice how these coincided, remembering their significance, and so resolving not to let ourselves slip away from faith in him for the future. We see how the government of Britain, and hence its people, was freed from the hands of the kings who would abuse their power. At the same time the monarchy became a safeguard of the nation by declaring that Protestant Christianity would be at the backbone of our legal system and that the Bible would be our guidebook. Interwoven with these remembrances are the wonderful deliverances which our nation has experienced, keeping us a sovereign nation with a history of Christian leadership and ministry to the world. On that basis we have been preserved and we have been secure.

Such was the heritage celebrated in 1988. In the Queen's speech that year she said:

> In the year just past, Prince Philip and I have joined in the celebrations of some notable anniversaries. The events which they marked were hundreds of years apart, but each was important enough to get much attention in 1988.
>
> The earliest event which we remembered was the encounter with the Spanish Armada in 1588. The 400th anniversary fell in the same year in which we were able to mark the happy relations between Britain and Spain which now exist, by our state visit to Madrid.
>
> Four hundred years after 'the winds blew' and the Spanish ships were scattered, the events were remembered, without animosity, in both countries. This year, the present King of Spain showed me the rooms in the Escorial, where his predecessor, Philip the Second, planned the campaign. Had the fortunes of war gone against us, how very differently events in Britain and Europe would have unfolded.
>
> Earlier in the year, we marked another event of the first importance in our history – the 300th anniversary of what is popularly known as the Glorious Revolution.
>
> The invitation to King William and Queen Mary to accept the thrones of England and Scotland finally laid to rest the 'enterprise of England' which Philip of Spain set in hand.
>
> It thus gave the particular direction to our history which was to lead to the development of parliamentary democracy and the tradition of political and religious toleration which Britain enjoys today.

In looking back in this way, we might easily call to mind many other interventions by God on behalf of the nation, and realise how much the hand of God has been upon us. 1988 marked seventy years since the victory of World War One. If one considers the deliverances of the Second World War, one remembers a nation that was called to prayer at times of emergency, and how God brought deliverance in answer to those prayers. For example, the nation was called to prayer on 26th May 1940, at the time just preceding the evacuation of the British Expeditionary Force from Dunkirk. More than 338,000 men were evacuated as God brought mighty miracles of deliverance. These came in several remarkable ways: God brought confusion to the German army, which halted its advance within ten miles of the British and Allied troops. The Luftwaffe was grounded because of a mighty storm. And then, by contrast, a great calm came to the English Channel at the time of the evacuation from the beaches by an armada of naval vessels and hundreds of civilian boats from Britain. Other deliverances which were acknowledged as being from the hand of God included the Battle of Britain, the defence of Malta and the campaigns in North Africa. During the war many Christians were praying step by step through the times of emergency. One such group was established at the Bible College of Wales in Swansea. The remarkable account of how God brought this group together for prayer is contained in a book entitled *Rees Howells, Intercessor*, published by Lutterworth Press. For those who are willing to study the way the hand of God has been upon the British nation over many centuries there is ample evidence, including these recent accounts which take us through the war years, up to the birth of the present generation. At the end of the Second World War both the Prime Minister and the King openly thanked God for our deliverance.

Thus have we been led to consider these things over the last few years, and we might suggest that God has brought them to remembrance for a purpose. He wants this nation to continue to honour him. We have not been perfect – far from it – but we have managed to stand firm on sound Christian truth and honour God at leadership level sufficiently to bring blessing and protection. If we were to consider the failures of our nation instead of our successes (as a nation will always fall short of perfection) we would be wise to respond to these things with humility, instead of which we are going headlong into ungodly behaviour that is an abomination to God.

God has placed men and women into nations. He has set our boundaries and he wants to build us up within those boundaries. This is why he will have particular things to say to the nation as a whole. In addition to the remembrances of the history of our nation and its Christian heritage, there is the most important remembrance of all, which is the foundation on which the rest is built. This is the gospel message itself, which can be summed up in the phrase, *Jesus is alive!*, the proclamation of which was carried as a postmark on Britain's mail during the Easter of 1988.

2

'Jesus Is Alive!' – The Story of a Postmark

> He placed his right hand on me and said: 'Do not be afraid. I am the First and the Last. I am the Living One; I was dead, and behold I am alive for ever and ever! And I hold the keys of death and Hades. Write, therefore, what you have seen, what is now and what will take place later' (Revelation 1:17–19).

Sunday after Sunday the gospel message still goes out from churches in every area of Britain. In addition there is always an interweaving of specialist evangelistic ministries among the congregations of Britain, and special works in many towns to declare the truths of the Bible and to bring help to the needy in practical outworkings of the gospel message.

There have been a number of national campaigns in which well-known preachers have spoken by various ways and means so that the whole nation can hear and respond to the call to repentance and salvation. Billy Graham has been well known and respected in Britain since the 1950s. He has preached a simple gospel message to thousands of people in stadiums across the nation and has spoken on radio and television. Others have addressed certain areas of the nation, such as when Luis Palau came to Wales in the 1980s to promote a campaign called 'Tell Wales'.

During 1994 various national evangelistic campaigns were held in the United Kingdom. In the months of February and March the pentecostal churches promoted a campaign entitled 'Jim' (meaning 'Jesus in me') as a national effort, designed to mobilise at least 1,000 local churches to make known the gospel message in their areas. The 'On Fire' campaign encouraged churches throughout the United Kingdom to unite and be involved in relevant evangelistic outreach over the May Pentecost weekend of 1994 and the two weeks following.

What has been described as the largest 'Gospel-Net' ever cast over the British Isles took place during the period from 14th to 31st March 1994. The vision behind this campaign was to take the message of the cross of Jesus and place it in every household in the British Isles and the Republic of Ireland. This message was placed in a gospel booklet entitled *Minus to Plus* by German evangelist Reinhard Bonnke, and the objective was to deliver this to 25 million homes. Those who responded to the message would be given a further booklet suitable for new Christians and put directly in touch with their local church for follow up and nurture in the faith. The follow-up booklet was called *The Ultimate Plus*. Churches were invited to register with 'Minus to Plus' so that they could follow up those who responded to the booklet in their area and, by the time the booklets were distributed, 15,400 churches and meeting places had registered. The total money received for this campaign was £4.2 million of which 93% came from the United Kingdom and the rest from other countries.

If we believe that God has inspired these campaigns we must realise that it is for a purpose. This is surely because there is an urgency rising in the heart of God for the people of Britain who, having had such a wonderful Christian heritage, are slipping away. It is a crisis like at other times of history when God has sent forth his word to bring repentance and deliverance.

'Jesus is alive!'

Because one of the authors of this book was involved in another national campaign we will describe this in some detail. There is a sense in which we see the present book as the next step on from this campaign to promote the message *Jesus is alive!* to the nation. The story stands as a testimony to God's love, faithfulness, guidance and provision. We are ordinary people ourselves, caught up as much as anyone in the ordinary life of this nation. We did not choose to write this book or to promote a postmark. While being very concerned about the decline of the nation, we are simply seeking to be obedient to God. This must be borne in mind as the testimony of the postmark is considered. It is not that a man wanted to do this, but that God asked a willing servant to do it. Indeed, you will always find a time of challenge within the prophetic ministry when the prophet just does not want to do what he is asked, out of his humanity. This is being said so that readers will catch the essence of our appeal to this nation to listen to what God is saying and turn to him. Our appeal is to the British people from God himself.

The year 1994, having a number of prominent evangelists in the United Kingdom was the beginning of the seventh year after the postmark campaign. Seven is a number which is important in the Bible, being the symbol of perfection and holiness. It is a number associated with rest (the seventh day or Sabbath and the sabbatical year). Seven sevens of years led to the year of Jubilee, a year of special favour and return to the Lord as well as cancelling of debts in human transactions. In the seventh month of the biblical calendar comes Yom Kippur, the Day of Atonement, an awesome day for repentance and turning to the Lord. These times and seasons do have significance within the plans of God, though we very often fail to notice God's timing. It is interesting to note that the Post Office issued four special stamps on St David's Day, 1st March 1988, to mark the 400th anniversary of the translation of the Bible into Welsh, perfectly coinciding with the issue of the postmark '*Jesus is alive!*' which ran from 1st March to 11th April 1988. Again, 1994 marked the 500th anniversary of the birth of William Tyndale. His life was one of persecution and in the end he suffered a martyr's death, being strangled and burned near Brussels in 1536. Yet he gave his life to the translation of the Bible into English and opened the way for the much prized Authorised Version of 1611 which gave all English-speaking men and women access to the Scriptures.

Such memories intertwine as a major sign to this nation and should be considered in the background to the testimony of Paul Slennett in proclaiming the message *Jesus is alive!* across the nation in 1988. What more effective way could God have chosen to send this message to the nation at the time of Easter, when the remembrance of Jesus' sacrificial and atoning death on the cross at Calvary would be remembered in all Christendom, than to have it put through the door of every home on the envelopes that were being delivered by the postmen of Britain?

The origins of the postmark were quiet and small. But they developed into a campaign of national proportions, being taken up by the media in all its forms, becoming an issue for debate in the country and even throughout the world. Those who have studied the consequences of the prophetic words of God will realise that this is a normal pattern. In this case, three words became an issue for national debate in an unprecedented way.

A national authority on postmarks, Tim Whitney, the author of *Collect British Postmarks*, assembled newspaper cuttings and other evidence which followed the campaign and wrote an account in August 1988. In the preface to the booklet he wrote:

> ... the row which erupted over the 'Jesus is Alive!' slogan in March/April 1988 is without precedent in British Postal History. Never before has a postmark been featured by television, radio, the British national and local press as well as newspapers overseas. When else has a postmark appeared on car stickers, T-shirts and balloons?

This simple idea, which conveyed the message of the fundamental truth of Christianity, not only arrived like an Easter message from God through the letterboxes of Britain and around the world, but it stirred up response in many ways. It could be said that it exposed the heart of Britain. Once this message would have been accepted as true and a means of blessing, but suddenly reaction erupted like a sleeping monster coming awake, as national figures debated the issues which it raised.

The story began in December 1984 when Tim Whitney visited a church where Paul Slennett, a Christian bookseller, was in attendance. He spoke to the children and made reference to his hobby of collecting British postmarks. Suddenly the thought came to Paul: 'Wouldn't it be good to have a Christian postmark?' He began to think about that and prayed, that if it was God's idea, he would bring it back one day when he wanted him to do something about it.

Paul's attitude was that even one prayer prayed in the will of God would be answered, and he was able to leave it like that. He did not pray about it again and did not even think about it. In July 1986, Paul attended a Christian conference, called 'Acts 86', at the National Exhibition Centre in Birmingham. Travelling in each day to the meetings he was captivated by some large signs containing the bold proclamation, 'Jesus is Lord'. The thought came perhaps he should buy one of them and put it on the front of his bookshop in Southend, proclaiming, 'Jesus is Lord!'.

So this led to questioning prayer, but he felt that the answer was that this was not the way to go, because it would lead to only the people of Southend seeing the message, while he sensed that the Lord wanted the whole nation to hear the message. 'How then,' asked Paul, 'can this message go to the whole nation? What vehicle could be used?' It was at this point that the Holy Spirit of God dropped just one word into Paul's mind. That word was 'postmark'. God was going to bring this about, a nationwide proclamation through a simple postmark. This was an awesome revelation, and one that Paul was powerless to bring about in his own strength. He began to pray for guidance and also made contact again with Tim Whitney, the expert on postmarks. Tim Whitney gave the sound advice needed in order to apply to the right people concerning Royal Mail postmarks.

That was the beginning of the process. Next Paul enquired of God concerning what the message was to be. This did not clarify immediately, but eventually it became clear that the message was to be 'Jesus is alive!' alongside which was to be a symbol of the empty cross, because Jesus has risen. A Christian printer designed various options from which the choice was made. The inclusion of the exclamation mark was considered important, because of the truly amazing truth that Jesus is alive today.

The very strict criteria for postmarks issued by the Post Office had to be considered. It was allowable to mark a national event with a postmark, so Paul was able to request that the national event of Easter was to be marked by this particular postmark, a Christian event with public holidays. Paul enquired about the postmark going out throughout Essex.

The prayer fellowship, Intercessors for Britain, visited Southend in September of 1987. This group, together with other Christian organisations, was discovered to be calling for a day of repentance and prayer in the nation on Saturday 5th March 1988. This provided confirmation of the proposed timing of the postmark. Shortly afterwards, in November, the idea was also tested with the editor of the magazine *Prophecy Today*. Intercessors for Britain and the committee calling for the national day of repentance and prayer gave support for the idea of the postmark. Paul was contacted by them in December of that year and asked to consider making it a nationwide rather than regional campaign.

There were financial implications: an Essex campaign would require £3,000; a nationwide campaign would cost around £50,000. Paul counted the cost of this commitment, and others from praying groups continued to confirm that the postmark should go nationwide. Paul began to enter into a contractual relationship with the Post Office in early January of 1988, with questions still remaining about how it would all be paid for. In fact it would have to be prepaid before the postmark could be sent out.

In July of 1987 there was an unexpected income of £10,000 to the Southend bookshop; it appeared to be provision from God. In September of the same year another £10,000 became available. With this extra £20,000, the remaining mortgage relating to the bookshop was paid off. This meant that when the £50,000 was needed for the postmark, Paul had a building with no mortgage which could stand as surety for a loan from a bank; and so the money was obtained. Paul explained to the bank manager that he believed that God would quickly pay off this debt.

Interestingly, the newspapers who reported on the postmark gave the impression that Paul had paid the money himself and that there was no debt to be recovered, but he believed that it was right not to make any appeals for money. Since God knew, he would provide. In fact the debt was paid within three months of the postmark, by June of 1988, partly from the shop's Christmas trading, and the rest from unsolicited gifts from all around the country.

The response begins

The reaction of the national press was truly remarkable, increasing the prominence of the message '*Jesus is alive!*' in ways that money could not have bought. There were three main stories. One was the launch of the postmark. Secondly, there were remarks by prominent leaders, including the Archbishop of Canterbury, Robert Runcie, who thought that the postmark was insensitive. Thirdly, the Methodists were trying to arrange a postmark to commemorate the Wesleys. Because of the outrage against the '*Jesus is Alive!*' postmark the Methodists were asked to change their postmark so that it did not contain a Christian message. The '*Jesus is Alive!*' postmark ran for six weeks and stirred up reaction throughout that time.

Remarkably, the Post Office honoured the contract to print it from their offices for the whole period (they had the option to withdraw it at any time) even with the reaction coming in from across the nation. Paul believes that God himself lifted the message into prominence. He did not plan that the national press and news media would respond as they did, but they heard of it and contacted him. Two UK television companies visited his shop to interview him. One interviewer asked how he could justify spending £50,000 on a postmark. Paul's reply was that if one person came to the Lord through the postmark then it would have been worth it. As he thought about it afterwards he realised that what he said was so true, for what is the value of a human soul? 'God so loved the world that he gave his one and only Son . . . .' This is the truth behind the proclamation, and the Lord would have done as much for just one person.

Many people contacted Paul from all over the world, including the ABC news network from the USA. There was an interview and Paul asked when the news item would go out. He was told that within a quarter of an hour it would be going coast to coast across America. This was the power of God, who could take a small postmark and use it to proclaim a message across America as well as Britain. The postmark was put on the front page of national newspapers – advertising space that would have cost many times the £50,000 – and every home had a personal message from God on their envelopes during Easter 1988. Indeed, across the whole world, this message went out to every country. The only country that returned letters with this postmark was the Muslim nation of Saudi Arabia.

The postmark, as well as drawing response from Christian leaders, also brought responses from other prominent people in the nation. It was a subject for discussion on the popular current affairs programme *Any Questions*. Among the telling responses was one from Bernard Levin who wrote in his column in *The Times* newspaper on 7th March 1988, under the title 'When franking incenses':

> Here I must once again pause for my familiar disclaimer. I am not a Christian, and have no *locus standi* from which to pronounce on Christian beliefs. If I *had* to answer the question implied in the notorious envelope-frank, I think that on balance – a very fine balance, in which the scale turns so slightly as to be to all intents imperceptible – I would have to say yes . . .

Up and down the country over the Christian celebration of Easter, the nation seemed to wake up to the challenge and the invitation that the statement

'Jesus is alive!' invoked. The message was on more than two hundred million envelopes and opened out debate in all walks of life.

The national press gave a mixed but overall negative response to the postmark. Most of their readers' letters were critical. British humanists were outraged. *The Guardian* newspaper reported that the British Humanist Association said the scheme was 'absolutely outrageous', and had written to the Chairman of the Post Office asking him to cancel it. Concern was expressed in some newspapers about offence to other faiths. Despite the generally negative public response, however, most of the hundreds of letters received privately thanked Paul for the initiative. Some even wrote movingly of the effect of the slogan at a time of bereavement.

Even today, several years after the postmark went out, fresh stories of its results come in now and again from around the world. Recently, a letter came from India with information about new Christian ministries that were inspired and grew as a result of the postmark. Just as in days gone by, we see that the Christian message can go out from Britain as an inspiration to nations where we once sent our missionaries. Surely we must say that God sent out that message to a nation that is on the verge of forgetting the message, and also to remind us that we have survived and prospered for so long because this truth was accepted and written into the fabric of our society.

Before the postmark went out, Paul Slennett wanted to inform Christian organisations and the Christian media about what was to take place. He began to compose a letter to send to them. Having written the letter he stayed up late one night to pray about its contents. In fact he found himself staying up all night and by the morning he felt that God had revealed to him that there was an addition to the letter to be made. The word 'woe' came to mind. The word 'woe' is often used in the Bible to speak of something which will turn out to be bad news to an individual or nation. Paul felt that there was to be a statement, with three 'woes', to be put into the letter. He had no understanding why there should be three 'woes' and would have really preferred to put just one 'woe'. It sounded rather different from the way he would normally speak, and three woes are only mentioned once in the whole Bible, in the Book of Revelation. All other instances are singular. Paul felt the Lord God constrain him to put in this letter to the Christian media:

> Woe! Woe! Woe! to this nation if it refuses to accept his proclamation that 'Jesus is Alive!' and that he died on the cross for our sins that we might be forgiven.

Paul finally went to bed at 5 am and told his wife that the Lord had just ruined his letter! He thought he might be ridiculed over those three 'woes' but decided to be obedient, and risk 'being a fool for Christ'. As it happened, no one from the Christian media picked up on this expression of the three woes, but it has become the foundation of the prophecy which gave rise to this book, and which will be explored in the next chapter.

We have given a short account of the remarkable testimony concerning the postmark in a way that would not normally be made known. We want to explain what is happening in the clearest terms, giving people as much information as we can, in order that they might consider carefully what God is saying to this nation. We believe he was reminding us of our Christian heritage and encouraging us to accept the gospel message, or face the consequences of rejecting him, which could be three woes.

He is not about to bring forth woes like some tyrant. He is sending warnings of judgement in order to cause people to turn to him. We have been shown the truth that Jesus is alive, and it is only on account of that truth that we can come to God for forgiveness of sins, for help in this life and security in the life to come.

We trust that, just as the postmark containing three simple words was raised up by God to send a message to the nation, so he will also make the coming judgement known. The details in this chapter show how he can do this. The response to the postmark was generally negative – a fact that must be remembered at the time of the coming earthquake when many may not find it easy to believe that God has sent it.

3

Judgement over Britain

> There will be great earthquakes, famines and pestilences in various places, and fearful events and great signs from heaven (Luke 21:11).

The prophecy

On Monday 6th February 1989 Paul Slennett went to the Hayes Conference Centre in Derbyshire to attend the Leaders' Prayer and Bible Week of Intercessors for Britain. This brought together Christians from all parts of the British Isles to pray for Britain. The organisation takes an active interest in the whole framework of national life, and is concerned for the growing ungodliness and falling away from biblical standards. Their response is chiefly in prayer, that evil might be exposed and the nation turn to the ways of God.

It was at this gathering that Paul received the prophecy concerning a mighty earthquake which would shake the economic system of Great Britain. One morning at the beginning of the week, he woke suddenly at about 1 am with the words 'My children, the alarm bells are sounding all over Europe' ringing in his ears.

His immediate response was to write the words down. As he did so, God began to dictate a complete message. The following is the complete and unchanged text of what was written that morning:

> My children, the alarm bells are sounding all over Europe, for judgement is being spoken out over the nations. Over your nation, Great Britain, a mighty earthquake is about to occur, an earthquake that will swallow up the whole City. Whole companies and city institutions will collapse in this earthquake, some never to rise again.
>
> My judgement that has been withheld for so long must now be unleashed on your nation in order that my church repent and lead this nation in repentance, for I am a Righteous and Holy God, just in all my ways, a God who longs to show mercy, but one who will no longer tolerate the unrighteousness of my dear church. It is out of love that I visit this nation with judgement – you must know that this must always be the case. My children, repent now before it is too late, for already the day of my return draws near and you must not be found wanting, like the virgins who did not fill their lamps with oil; but awake, my children, and be my watchmen, and speak with a prophetic voice of the judgement that is about to come upon the nations.
>
> If you repent and turn from your wicked ways, I will visit your nation, Great Britain, once again, not with judgement, but with revival power, and I will protect you from all the strategy of the enemy.
>
> In regard to Europe, come out of her, my dear children, for she will align herself with the Beast and the False Prophet who will arise and appear for just a short while. My children, take heart, for I am with you always. Do not give up, but pray without ceasing and see the salvation of your God.

After writing this down, Paul asked God to confirm the prophetic message and to show that it was truly from him. He knew that a prophecy must be tested. He went back to sleep, waking just once more at 3 am, when God added to Paul's understanding that the reason these things were coming on the nation was because the church is asleep.

The confirmation

By a series of events which then followed, confirmation of the prophecy began to come. Paul was reticent to share the prophecy with the leaders the following morning. However, he did tell one of those involved with the Intercessors for Britain leadership what had happened, who later passed it on to the leaders of the organisation. There was something of confirmation in the morning Bible teaching; without knowing about the prophecy, the Bible teacher spoke on a theme which echoed the final words of the prophecy: 'Take heart. Do not give up, but pray without ceasing.'

The Bible makes it clear that there will be troubles in this world. Believers in Jesus Christ do not escape these troubles, but maturity is reached by persevering through trials. At such times God will often inspire his preachers, pastors and teachers to exhort believers to persevere and to remind them of his ways. He requires us to pray at all times and to bring our needs and circumstances to him.

Later came further confirmation: all over Europe, during the period of this prayer and Bible conference, there were extreme and unusual weather patterns. The conference leadership suggested that these were the 'alarm bells' spoken of in the prophecy. On 7th February, while London had its warmest February day for eighteen years, being as warm as Bahrain and warmer than Majorca and Tunis, the rest of Europe was covered with smog, with alarmingly high pollution levels. In cities all over Europe poisonous fumes, particularly from cars, were trapped at ground level by unusual atmospheric conditions. This was so bad that consideration was given to banning certain vehicles from the roads. On 8th February Italy suffered extreme flooding, as did Scotland, where torrential storms carried away a bridge in Inverness. London continued in brilliant sunshine; Venice faced its worst drought in living memory, and there were snow reports at the Equator and on the Canary Islands. On 9th February a tornado hit Madrid accompanied by hailstones, while in Scotland the River Ness nearly burst its banks and, by contrast, a drought was announced in Surrey and Kent.

To those who find it hard to understand that God sends signs through the weather, we would say that this is in agreement with both recent experience and the teaching of the Bible. God is still able and willing to use signs and judgements within the created order, as we will see in Chapter 7 when we consider the 1987 hurricane in Britain, and when we consider the message of the Bible prophets. One of these was Amos. He said these things to Israel at a time of judgement:

> 'I also withheld rain from you when the harvest was still three months away. I sent rain on one town, but withheld it from another. One field had rain; another had none and dried up. People staggered from town to town for water but did not get enough to drink, yet you have not returned to me,' declares the Lord (Amos 4:7–8).

God spoke in this way to Israel through Amos his prophet, and the history of that nation confirms that God acted according to his word. Israel is a nation with a special covenant with God. However, God intended us to learn from his dealings with Israel – about his word, his ways and his works. Britain entered voluntarily into its own covenant with God through the Coronation Oath, so we should expect him from time to time to use the same means of communication with us as he did with Israel. This is surely what he is doing, even in the weather, and we should be able to interpret the signs, because our nation has a rich biblical heritage.

While the sermon was being preached at the conference, God spoke further to Paul, revealing that through this prophecy he was announcing the first of three woes. This recalled to mind the sentence Paul had inserted in his letter at the time of the postmark. Only the first woe has been made known to us: a mighty earthquake will hit the economic structure of the nation. The second and third woes will only take place if we fail to respond to the first in the right way.

A personal judgement

Later in the year, an incident took place in Paul's life which emphasised the reality of what can happen when economic problems occur. It also demonstrates that anyone can be affected by the economic shaking which is to come, including Christians. What happened also shows how a physical sign can accompany a financial judgement. The experience of believers is that God can and will deliver us out of difficulties, but Paul and his family had to persevere through this trial and reap the consequences of the woe that came upon them. This will be the pattern for many of us, so what we will describe next has warnings for many people from all walks of life, as well as the leaders of national institutions and companies. The chief warning is about debt which has come about by covetousness. When debts are called in at a time of financial crisis, for some people there will result personal or corporate bankruptcy, and the distress which this brings.

Around the time that the prophecy was given, Paul and his family were contemplating a house move. They owned a small four bedroomed house but wanted to move to a different area and were attracted by a larger and more expensive house. Their motives for the move itself seemed to be sound – to move closer to good schools and to the church they were attending. However, Paul made the mistake of saying that he would only move if it was to a better house. He now recognises that his motives were not pure. In fact, the move proved to be very difficult, because they could not sell their original house. The family's life savings were used and the balance was borrowed, on the assumption that the bulk of this would be paid back when the original house was sold. The move took place in July 1989 while their first house was still on the market.

Three things then happened simultaneously, all in the same month, which was like a financial earth tremor to the family. First, the Chancellor put up interest rates to a record level. Secondly, house prices collapsed. Thirdly, there was a sudden dramatic subsidence in the foundations of the wall of the garage of the new house. A wall, extending from their garage to their neighbour's adjoining garage, simply sank into the ground, leaving a gap right across, where the upper portion has separated from the lower portion.

The result of all this was that the unsold house went down in value by £15,000 and still did not sell, and the larger house could not be sold due to the subsidence. To add to the problems, the neighbour's house, which was already suffering from subsidence, then incurred additional damage due to strong winds the following January. The wall of the main bedroom collapsed. The rebuilding of the neighbour's house and garage, together with Paul's garage, made the sale of the larger house impossible. Meanwhile, the family debt was rising due to deferred interest.

The rebuilding of the neighbour's house together with Paul's garage led to a full three and a half years of woe. Then the larger house was sold and the family moved back to the first house. The financial consequences were that all of the family savings were lost and the enormous accumulated debt had to be paid.

One can only imagine the effect of this financial difficulty on the family, but many people could be trapped in this sort of way in our debt-laden society. Paul's initial response was to lose heart; he felt like giving up and did not know how to pray. Here is an important lesson. This is the natural way to respond when the foundations of our life are shaken. But Paul realised his error, both in the wrong motives of the house transactions and in regard to repentance. He had sinned, but now recognised his sin, as King David had done in his adultery with Bathsheba, and just as God told King David that he could not keep the fruit of his sin, namely, the baby that was to be born, so Paul could not keep the object of his sin, namely the house. He felt that God said to him, 'Will you trust the housing market to get you out of trouble or trust me?' This brought the family to prayer and the house then sold at a tremendous loss. Eventually, due to God's faithfulness and mercy, financial stability returned.

Paul felt that he had learned a lesson that will apply to many people when the financial shaking comes to the nation. Sin and failing to seek God's guidance were the reasons for the financial problems and this led to deep trouble when the collapse came suddenly. However, God was faithful and responded to confession and repentance. When a financial collapse hits this nation there will be many consequences to face for many people and it will not be easy, but the right response will be to turn in faith and repentance to God, who will help. Paul also felt that, in the collapsing of the wall of his garage, God was also saying that our lives need to be built on the right foundations, and that this applies to both the nation and to individuals.

The Bible warns clearly about the disasters which can befall us when our business is done in sinful ways. Just as Paul Slennett's day of reckoning came so it will be for many others when disaster strikes suddenly.

> Woe to him who builds his palace by unrighteousness, his upper rooms by injustice, making his countrymen work for nothing, not paying them for their labour. He says, 'I will build myself a great palace with spacious upper rooms.' So he makes large windows in it, panels it with cedar and decorates it in red (Jeremiah 22:13–14).

> Woe to him who piles up stolen goods and makes himself wealthy by extortion! How long must this go on? Will not your debtors suddenly arise? Will they not wake up and make you tremble? Then you will become their victim (Habakkuk 2:6–7).

> Woe to him who builds his realm by unjust gain to set his nest on high (Habakkuk 2:9).

> But everyone who hears these words of mine and does not put them into practice is like a foolish man who built his house on sand. The rain came down, the streams rose, and the winds blew and beat against that house, and it fell with a great crash (Matthew 7:26–27).

Paul and Clifford met for the first time in the Autumn of 1990 at a Christian retreat centre in Suffolk, where Clifford was the invited speaker at a day of seminars to consider the rise and challenge of Islam in the UK. During dinner they began to discuss the state of the nation in more general terms, which led to a further private meeting later in the evening when they talked together about the prophecy for the first time. In no way did Paul intend to write the account in a book, and efforts were made to ask other people to pass on the message of the prophecy. However, it was from that point on that it became gradually clear that one way for the prophecy to be made known was through a book. This conviction grew over the years as they met and prayed together and corresponded by letter and telephone.

Clifford felt an immediate sense of the importance of the prophecy and was filled with an awesome sense of the urgency of the time for Britain. It so happened that he was one of the invited guests to the National Prayer Breakfast at Westminster later in the year. This was a gathering of some of the Members of the House of Commons and House of Lords, together with Christian leaders of the nation just before Parliament re-opened in the Autumn. These leaders come together each year to pray for the nation and for

Parliament. When he attended this prayer gathering on 21st November 1990, Clifford felt the urgency of the prophecy burning within him, but there was no easy opportunity to bring it to the attention of the gathering during the formal proceedings. Later, he wondered if he should have made an effort to share the prophecy, and he subsequently wrote to the organisers of the prayer breakfast, who considered it and passed it on to the Lord Chancellor. At the time, however, Clifford simply prayed that God would do anything necessary in order to turn this nation to himself and his fatherly love. Many of the assembled dignitaries said 'Amen' to this prayer. Of course, in praying, Clifford had in mind that the prophecy would come about and that it would be God's means of turning the nation back to himself.

The very next day, on 22nd November, Margaret Thatcher, the then Prime Minister, made it known that she was resigning from her leadership position. Now, Margaret Thatcher's replacement as Prime Minister does not imply that she alone was under the judgement of God and accountable for all the sins of the nation, but a train of events was set in motion which will lead up to the financial collapse.

4

Blessings and Woes: The Biblical Pattern

> When a trumpet sounds in a city, do not the people tremble? When disaster comes to a city, has not the Lord caused it? (Amos 3:6).

The Bible is an account of the history of the world, from the beginning to the end. In the first book, Genesis, we learn of the fall of mankind through the sin of Adam. In the last book, Revelation, we read of the coming final judgement on the earth, when Jesus Christ returns. The chief emphasis of the Bible is the recovery plan which God implemented to bring back fallen and sinful mankind into a relationship with him – the relationship of a father with his child. The path of recovery focuses on one particular nation that God chose to teach his ways for this life and to focus his plans for the kingdom of heaven: the nation of Israel.

The climax of the plan of salvation was the sacrificial death of the Lord Jesus Christ on a cross at Calvary outside the city walls of Jerusalem. In accordance with the teaching of God through the prophets, a sacrifice would be given of this perfect Lamb of God to pay for the sins of the whole world. This is the gospel message. It is not for Israel alone, but for anyone of any generation who will believe in Jesus, who rose from the dead and is now sitting at the right hand of the Father in heaven.

While we are in this world, the principles by which to live, which please God, are laid out in the chapters of the Bible. They are principles which were first taught to Israel, but are now made known, through the Bible, to all people. These principles are very simple in one way, but deeply meaningful in another. For example, the book of Leviticus, which contains many of God's laws, has a chapter which is very brief (chapter 25), but it contains principles of economics which could set the foundations of any economic system. At first, these principles seem to have applied to Israel as they entered the land of Canaan, but they could be adapted to any generation in any country. They cover things like fair rent, care of the poor, ownership and responsibility. Above all, they show that it is both possible and necessary to organise our economies in a way which God himself can bless.

Similarly, for the management of our affairs, including the family and the care and education of our children, and national government, God set a perfect pattern before Israel which could be passed on to any generation and any nation of the world. Following these principles is not easy – Israel failed on many counts – but they are the basis on which any country can try to honour God. Doing this will not lead to the salvation of any nation for eternity, but it will provide a framework within which God can bless us on this earth.

We learn through God's dealings with Israel that

we can choose which route we follow. We can choose the route of blessing in covenant with him, or we can go our own way. When our own way takes us away from God's principles, then we have chosen the path which will eventually lead to judgement. For one thing, when we walk out of God's protection we will make mistakes which will bring us troubles. For another, there will come a day when all ungodliness on this earth will be judged. If we have not sought forgiveness through the atoning blood of Jesus Christ while we are on this earth, then we will be answerable for all our sins.

The immensity of God's judgements is to be seen in the way he destroyed the cities of Sodom and Gomorrah at the time of Abraham (see Genesis 19), for the abominations of their sins. We see the devastation that came to the whole earth during the flood at the time of Noah (Genesis 6–8). When wickedness becomes rampant, the most holy God will act to erase it from the face of the earth.

God's chosen people

Israel was the special covenant nation, and they knew God's particular judgements when they fell into sin. Much was expected of them, for they were raised up by God to demonstrate his ways to the whole world. The history of Israel, therefore, is a history of blessings and woes. We are meant to study these things in order to come into our own covenant relationship with God, so that we can be counted among his special people. Normally, God's people are individuals scattered among all nations, and it is unusual for a nation as a whole to come into a special agreement with God.

However, Britain has succeeded in doing this through its national leadership, based on the Coronation Oath. The leaders of our nation have been committed to leading the people according to the true Christian faith by a vow taken by the monarch before God at each coronation.

Thus, in a certain way, we are a covenant nation, or at least we attempted to be. We do not replace Israel and so we must be careful to understand that God must make of this covenant what he will. Yet we have received blessings and have had opportunities like few other nations to bless the world. So it is reasonable to argue that God will send warnings and judgements to us, as he did to Israel, at times when we are falling away from our covenant. As with Sodom and Gomorrah, God has judgements for all communities who rise up in ungodly ways, particularly when they have refused to accept the gospel message of the Lord Jesus Christ. As in the time of Noah, God will one day judge the whole world – not by water but by fire (see 2 Peter 3). However, we will also see signs and judgements throughout our history as the gospel of salvation is preached and God raises up witnesses to declare his will and his ways.

This is the reason we should study the messages of the prophets of the Bible and God's dealings with Israel: they are relevant to us in Britain as we come to a time of profound judgement. God is perfect love, but he cannot and will not compromise his holiness. As Creator of the universe, he has immense power and his judgements can make the universe shake. When we lose our sense of awe and right fear of God, we are in danger of forgetting what he has done and can still do. The judgement on Sodom and Gomorrah, which included judgement of sexual sin, brought burning sulphur from heaven to consume the cities and all the people. The flood covered the whole earth, wiping out all creatures that breathe from the land, including all mankind, except Noah's family and the animals that went into the Ark. The whole earth felt the devastating judgement of God.

When Israel, God's chosen people, sinned, they were removed from their land. Yet even when God's judgements cast the nation of Israel into exile, the message of the prophets spoke of his unfailing love and his higher purposes:

> As a mother comforts her child, so will I comfort you; and you will be comforted over Jerusalem (Isaiah 66:13).

> For your Maker is your husband – the Lord Almighty is his name – the Holy One of Israel is your Redeemer; he is called the God of all the earth (Isaiah 54:5).

As we read the Bible we will learn of God's character as well as his judgements and we should then apply that knowledge to our present situation in Britain. For example there is a principle in 2 Chronicles 7: 13–14. When the Temple in Jerusalem was built, Solomon had prayed to God for protection and guidance, and God answered clearly with conditions for blessing. It was foreseen that there would be times of judgement ahead, but a way back was always on offer:

> When I shut up the heavens so that there is no rain, or command locusts to devour the land or send a plague among my people, if my people, who are called by my name, will humble themselves and pray and seek my face and turn from their wicked ways, then will I hear from heaven and will forgive their sin and will heal their land.

This message was given to Israel, but it contains a promise that is still in force to this day. So what of Britain? Surely we who have covenanted with God can see that his character is indeed to forgive and to restore us, but that will be after we have been judged and woes have besct us on account of our sins. Unless God receives our repentance before the earthquake. Then God, who is abounding in love, will apply these principles of recovery to us.

A time of shaking

In this book we are declaring that God *is* speaking to Britain, that he *is* about to pass judgement on us through the financial system, and that he will use a mighty earthquake. All these things accord with the revelation of the Bible. Indeed, Jesus said specifically that there would be earthquakes among the 'signs of the times':

> There will be great earthquakes, famines and pestilences in various places, and fearful events and great signs from heaven (Luke 21:11).

He was speaking of what would take place before his return to the earth, and records show that earthquake activity is increasing across the world.

He also said:

> As it was in the days of Noah, so it will be at the coming of the Son of Man. For in the days before the flood, people were eating and drinking, marrying and giving in marriage, up to the day Noah entered the ark; and they knew nothing about what would happen until the flood came and took them all away. That is how it will be at the coming of the Son of Man (Matthew 24:37–39).

Jesus gave us advance warning that there would come a time on this earth when we would be so caught up in the activities of this life that we would fail to recognise the signs of his coming. That will be a time of judgement comparable to the time of Noah's flood.

The witness of prophets like Haggai is that times of great 'shaking' can be physical as well as symbolic – earthquakes in the physical earth as well as collapsing world systems:

> I will shake the heavens and the earth. I will overturn royal thrones and shatter the power of the foreign kingdoms. I will overthrow chariots and their drivers; horses and their riders will fall, each by the sword of his brother (Haggai 2:21–22).

Just as a father takes a rebellious son by the lapels of his coat and shakes him firmly to bring him to his senses, so God will shake the world. In the New Testament Haggai's words are repeated, reminding us that everything, including our economies, will be shaken. The only things which will not topple under such shaking are the things built on the foundations of the word of God.

> See to it that you do not refuse him who speaks. If they did not escape when they refused him who warned them on earth, how much less will we, if we turn away from him who warns us from heaven? At that time his voice shook the earth, but now he has promised, 'Once more I will shake not only the earth but also the heavens.' The words 'once more' indicate the removing of what can be shaken – that is, created things – so that what cannot be shaken may remain. Therefore, since we are receiving a kingdom that cannot be shaken, let us be thankful, and so worship God acceptably with reverence and awe, for our 'God is a consuming fire' (Hebrews 12:25–29).

There is no doubt about the power of God to speak and cause the earth to tremble. Our only question is, when will he do this in our circumstances? We believe that these prophecies about the shaking across the nations to remove ungodly practice are now upon us, and we would be wise to consider this with godly fear.

Right economic principles

That the economy is a focus of God's blessings and woes is seen clearly in the words Moses passed on about how the people of Israel were to live in their Promised Land:

> And all these blessings will come upon you and accompany you if you obey the Lord your God: You will be blessed in the city and blessed in the country. The fruit of your womb will be blessed, and the crops of your land and the young of your livestock – the calves of your herds and the lambs of your flocks. Your basket and your kneading trough will be blessed. You will be blessed when you come in, and blessed when you go out (Deuteronomy 28:2–6).

These promises are capable of clear interpretation in any economy. They refer to the produce of the land, the things that we make or manufacture and the way our affairs are ordered. It might seem far-fetched to those who go their own way in this world, never conscious of the direct revelation or protection of God, that there is a God who can and will do these things. He will keep blight from our crops, preserve us from harsh weather conditions and send suitable weather in each season, lead us through the economic complexities of the world and cause us to prosper, but only if we live according to very simple Bible principles. But if we do not implement God's principles in our family, community and national life, if we decide to go our own way, then there will be woe rather than blessing:

> However, if you do not obey the Lord your God and do not carefully follow all his commands and decrees I am giving you today, all these curses will come upon you and overtake you: You will be cursed in the city and cursed in the country. Your basket and your kneading trough will be cursed. The fruit of your womb will be cursed and the crops of your land, and the calves of your herds and the lambs of your flocks. You will be cursed when you come in and cursed when you go out (Deuteronomy 28:15–19).

Britain today

These promises were for Israel, and their history demonstrates that they are true and valid. They are unlike any other nation in God's direct dealings. In the light of this, it is remarkable that Britain was able to achieve what she did through a voluntary covenant, and remarkable that she has in a measure felt these blessings. Now we are feeling the growing tide of curses and this coincides with a rise of ungodliness in our nation. Some of the curses mentioned in the list, though symbolic to some extent, have been literally fulfilled, like the curse on our cattle. We can attribute these things to chance, or we can understand that God himself is dealing with our nation.

Something quite remarkable happened in Britain to give the nation its Christian heritage. Perhaps we have not fully understood why God blessed us in this way. Perhaps we have taken our heritage for granted. Perhaps we have claimed for ourselves the honour that was due to God. Perhaps we thought we became world leaders by our own expertise and strength, preventing invasion, winning world wars, establishing successful organisations to care for our people, and so on. However, if we miss the point that it was God who helped us, then we come into grave danger. The time may come when the nation as a whole will *not* be under God's protection and blessing. Some people say, judging by the present decline in standards, that this time has already arrived. However, because of the prophecy we have been given, our belief is that we are being warned rather than abandoned.

People who have known peace and prosperity may find it difficult to imagine what it could be like when God's blessing and protection are removed. Yet there is no reason why Britain could not slip gradually into the condition of many of the other countries of the world. If we decide to follow false gods of those nations then we will come under the same curses as them. We will know what it is like to be abandoned by the true God. Perhaps, in such a situation, the church itself could grow in spiritual strength, perhaps underground, perhaps persecuted, but the nation as a whole would become utterly forsaken by God as it went its own sinful, proud way.

God is slow to anger and abounding in love. He is far more patient with us than we realise, and so these things do not happen at the first signs of error. The time will come, however, when all warnings have been given and judgement will fall. Now is the time to repent of our sins and let God rebuild us. The sins of recent years are piling up before God and our condition requires urgent attention.

The reason we can understand that the times are urgent for Britain is because we can study in the Bible the patterns of God's dealings with Israel. This was the nation that God chose first and taught his ways, but also warned that blessings would only follow for obedience to his commands. The Ten Commandments contain the foundational teaching and the whole of the Bible contains other teaching which flows from these commandments. Obedience to these commandments does not save us for the next life; salvation only comes through spiritual rebirth. But obedience to the commandments brings blessings. Britain needs leaders of the nation and of the church who will teach us these things again.

We must also consider the rise and fall of all the major empires of the world. Babylon, Persia, Greece and Rome all rose to world dominance and fell to nothing during and shortly after Bible times. No empire has lasted, even though it reached almost irresistible strength at certain times. More recently we have seen the British Empire rise and fall. Communism has come and gone. Nations and powers may rise for a short time, but they do not continue for ever. Other powers will rise and subdue them. This will continue to be the pattern of history.

Within the rise and fall of empires we can consider how they responded to God's laws. When we do, we see that there has been none like Britain. True, America has grown as a Christian witness. The blessings for America were once an overspill of the blessings of Britain. Now she is independent, but even America does not have the same covenant with God as we, in Britain, have expressed in the Coronation Oath. Europe may seem to be rising in power, but it is not setting out to keep covenant with God, so will not be a union that is blessed.

Britain is vulnerable. She made a covenant with God and is breaking it by reversing the laws which once were inspired by the commandments of God in the Bible, and there is much sin in the nation. She is not the nation of Israel, though she has known some of the blessings once promised to Israel. Yet, if Israel lost her blessings for doing less than Britain is today, in not obeying the commandments, how long will God continue to bless us? In the days in which we live, the signs are that evil is rising in the world and we are warned to keep out of ungodly alliances. God is speaking to us and he could continue to bless us but we need to take radical action quickly. Jeremiah spoke a prophecy which is directly relevant for Britain today:

> If at any time I announce that a nation or kingdom is to be uprooted, torn down and destroyed, and if that nation I warned repents of its evil, then I will relent and not inflict on it the disaster I had planned. And if at another time I announce that a nation or kingdom is to be built up and planted, and if it does evil in my sight and does not obey me, then I will reconsider the good I had intended to do for it (Jeremiah 18:7–10).

The pattern of the Bible is that obedience to God's laws brings blessing, disobedience brings curse. God did not compromise this for the nation of Israel, so he will not compromise for any other nation. Yet Britain has been blessed. She is now under judgement and is likely to reap pain and suffering. In these days of immense world change, God is warning us to repent so that we might be blessed once more. This is possible from God's side, but is beginning to look improbable from ours unless we open our Bibles, and also look at our history, realising that God is in heaven and is waiting for our response. It is unlikely that this opportunity will last for a long time, and God's last words of invitation of blessing to Britain as a whole could come in the near future.

5

The Prophets Speak Today

> Surely the Sovereign Lord does nothing without revealing his plan to his servants the prophets (Amos 3:7).

All the prophets of the Bible have relevant messages for us which will encourage us to believe in God's judgements and to realise that a mighty earthquake which causes a financial collapse of the City is perfectly in line with God's ways and quite appropriate for the circumstances in Britain today. The prophet Amos is especially relevant. He prophesied to Israel two years before an earthquake (see Amos 1:1). He was an ordinary man whom God raised up to speak to a nation whose sins were wide-ranging in social, religious, and economic spheres, and he showed that God speaks through signs in the weather and through circumstances. We will look closely at what this book contains.

The book of Amos contains nine short chapters and takes up about ten pages of the Bible. Its message is brief but it is complete. It is a masterpiece of literature yet it was written by the hand of an ordinary labourer. When we read it, realising that God was the source of its inspiration, the words bring an awesome warning to any nation in the same situation as the Israel of Amos' day. The message echoes through history to present-day Britain.

We discover information on the condition of the kingdom of Israel, which had fallen into decline. We see the nature of the sins of the nation, and the signs that God had sent as warnings. We see how God addresses his warnings to the leaders, and how the judgements of God fall on the whole nation. We can also see how hard it can be for the voice of the prophet of God to be heeded but how, nevertheless, God's judgements come to pass.

The book of Amos contains clear parallels with Britain today. As it is read we can be conscious of the economic difficulties in our nation which accompany dishonesty in business and seeking after personal gain at the expense of others. We can be conscious of the decline in morals and other standards of the leadership of our nation and the consequent difficulties, including, for example, the break-up of marriages in the Royal Family. We can consider the signs in the weather as well as the shaking in the City.

Jeroboam the Second, the fourteenth king of the Northern Kingdom of Israel was in power, reigning from Samaria the capital city. He had come to power in the year 782 BC. This was around 150 years after King Solomon's death, when the Promised Land had split into the two kingdoms of Israel and Judah. These 150 years had seen both good and bad times. The good times coincided with God's blessings when God's laws were obeyed. The bad times followed God's judgements when God's laws were disobeyed. But in the times of judgement there was always a prophet to warn the people to return to God and his ways.

Jeroboam was not a good king: 'He did evil in the eyes of the Lord and did not turn away from any of the sins of Jeroboam son of Nebat, which he had caused Israel to commit' (2 Kings 14:24). In verse 26 of the same chapter we read, 'The Lord had seen how bitterly everyone in Israel, whether slave or free, was suffering; there was no-one to help them.' But the chapter goes on to say that the king, even though he promoted sin in the nation, was used as an instrument of God to help the people.

This is the nature of God. He sees how nations fall away from him because of bad leadership; he holds the leaders accountable; but he also delays any catastrophe on the nation itself. In compassion he withholds judgement and even uses a wrongly motivated leadership to help the needy. He sends warnings, both through signs and through the mouths of the prophets. In the final analysis everyone becomes answerable for their own sins, but God fully understands how a nation is led into error and he always has his eyes on the poor and needy.

God speaks

In about the year 760 BC, Amos, who worked in Tekoa, about twelve miles from Jerusalem, heard the voice of God. Amos was an ordinary farm labourer, a shepherd and tender of sycamore-fig trees. He was told to go from the Southern Kingdom of Judah to the Northern Kingdom of Israel with a warning (see Amos 1:1 and 7:14–15). Chapter 7 of Amos records how Amos was sent to Bethel. Here the worship of God had been replaced by the worship of idols in the form of calves. The priesthood had become corrupt, but it was not a religious leader who was raised up to prophesy to the king and to the nation, but a humble labourer.

Amaziah was the priest at Bethel and he tried to silence Amos and sent warnings to the king concerning what Amos was saying. The future monarch of Britain is open to the counsel of teachers of other faiths and would like to be Defender of Faith rather than Defender of *the* Faith. Defender of Faith is an ambiguous title that challenges the uniqueness of Jesus Christ as being the only way to God. Jesus said of himself, 'I am the way, the truth and the life. No-one comes to the Father except through me' (John 14:6). If Prince Charles compromises the Christian faith by adopting the title Defender of Faith, then there are awesome similarities between Britain and ancient Israel. According to the Coronation Oath of Britain, far from supporting the gods of other faiths, our monarch promises to lead the nation in submission to the God of the Bible, just as the kings of Israel were expected to do, and not to compromise with other gods and other religions.

The words of Amos to the priest of Bethel, to the king and to the nation were uncompromising. He confronted Amaziah with these words:

> Now then, hear the word of the Lord. You say, 'Do not prophesy against Israel, and stop preaching against the house of Isaac.' Therefore this is what the Lord says: 'Your wife will become a prostitute in the city, and your sons and daughters will fall by the sword. Your land will be measured and divided up, and you yourself will die in a pagan country. And Israel will certainly go into exile, away from their native land' (Amos 7:16–17).

We believe the Lord has a message for the leaders and people of the nation of Britain. When our sins are compared with Israel's in Amos' day, surely what he says will be carried out, just as it was in Amos' day. And just as in Amos' day, the leaders of the nation who are also Christians should sense a double warning. Another prophet, Hosea, spoke words that can also be interpreted in the context of Britain's decline (see Hosea 4:8–9). Hosea spoke to the priests of Israel who were encouraging the sins of the people through their leadership:

> They feed on the sins of my people and relish their wickedness. And it will be: Like people, like priests. I will punish both of them for their ways and repay them for their deeds.

Those who hold religious office in the leadership of a nation are under the same judgement as the nation. Christian leaders who know God's ways have an awesome responsibility when that nation departs from God's laws.

The principle of how God reveals his plans is clear from Amos 3:7: 'Surely the Sovereign Lord does nothing without revealing his plan to his servants the prophets.' We see from Amos how God can choose an unexpected person to be his mouthpiece. We also see that the words of the prophet can be rejected, particularly if he opposes the leadership. At times of judgement God demands repentance, and repentance involves an admission of error, and a turning to God's ways. Repentance demands humility and it may demand considerable change in the way we live. For Jeroboam it meant, among other things, the destruction of the idols of Bethel and the reformation of religious practices. It also demanded a change in the way the land was ruled. For Britain repentance will mean returning to laws that acknowledge God's ways, and for the leaders of the land openly to declare that they will lead the people to worship the only true God.

In the first two chapters of Amos we have brief sections on God's judgement on thc nations around Israel. God had noted everything that had been done in Damascus, Gaza, Tyre, Edom, Ammon, Moab and Judah. He saw all the injustice and was about to judge those nations. God still goes on observing all the nations of the world, watching to see if they are living according to his ways.

Israel should have known God's requirements better than any other nation: 'He has revealed his word to Jacob, his laws and decrees to Israel. He has done this for no other nation; they do not know his laws' (Psalm 147:19–20). When Amos' attention turned to Israel, therefore, after referring to the other nations, his words would have come like a hammer blow:

> 'They sell the righteous for silver, and the needy for a pair of sandals. They trample on the heads of the poor as upon the dust of the ground and deny justice to the oppressed. Father and son use the same girl and so profane my holy name. They lie down beside every altar on garments taken in pledge. In the house of their god they drink wine taken as fines. I destroyed the Amorite before them, though he was tall as the cedars and strong as the oaks. I destroyed his fruit above and his roots below. I brought you up out of Egypt, and I led you forty years in the desert to give you the land of the Amorites. I also raised up prophets from among your sons and Nazirites from among your young men. Is this not true, people of Israel?' declares the Lord. 'But you made the Nazirites drink wine and commanded the prophets not to prophesy' (Amos 2:6–12).

Israel was no longer governed by righteous principles. This had affected the economy of the land so that the poor were not treated fairly and justice no longer prevailed. Sexual immorality had grown to a shocking level and the religious establishment was in disorder. God reminded the people through Amos what he had done for them and now this is what he found: a corrupt nation.

The message for us too is clear: greed, dishonesty and sexual immorality are rampant in Britain. Justice is perverted. Behind the scenes of many of our institutions lies corruption and dishonesty. The message of Amos shows that God has seen it all: 'Surely the eyes of the Sovereign Lord are on the sinful kingdom' (Amos 9:8). Nothing is hidden from him. Just as Israel could look back and be reminded of God's provision, teaching and deliverance, so can Britain. Britain has known the laws of God because preachers of God's word through many generations have led the people into God's truth. Britain has known the prosperity of a nation kept by God himself. We have been delivered from the hands of many tyrants who seemed like giants to us at the time. Deliverance from the Nazi tyranny is within living memory, but history is full of such deliverances for our nation. So we can read the words of Amos, spoken once to Israel, and apply them to ourselves.

The judgement comes

> 'Now then, I will crush you as a cart crushes when loaded with grain. The swift will not escape, the strong will not muster their strength, and the warrior will not save his life. The archer will not stand his ground, the fleet-footed

> soldier will not get away, and the horseman will not save his life. Even the bravest warriors will flee naked on that day,' declares the Lord (Amos 2:13–16).

When God rises up to judge there is nothing that can withstand his judgements. The strongest of men, who have trained and honed their muscles for a lifetime, will wilt to nothing before the strength of the Lord. He can raise up and he can bring down. The greatest of institutions will collapse under his judgements – even the economy. When God judges, it is not in the natural strength or ability of man to find a way out.

> You who turn justice into bitterness and cast righteousness to the ground . . . though you have built stone mansions, you will not live in them; though you have planted lush vineyards, you will not drink their wine. For I know how many are your offences and how great your sins. You oppress the righteous and take bribes and you deprive the poor of justice in the courts. Therefore the prudent man keeps quiet in such times, for the times are evil (Amos 5:7–13).

Evil they are, indeed, in Britain today, and God, who created all of the universe, is noting our transgressions. Judgement will be the inevitable consequence. 'When a trumpet sounds in a city, do not the people tremble? When disaster comes to a city, has not the Lord caused it?' (Amos 3:6). Amos could be speaking directly to the economic centre of the City of London today. And why? 'Because they have rejected the law of the Lord and have not kept his decrees, because they have been led astray by false gods' (Amos 2:4).

The remedy is also to be found in Amos:

> Seek good, not evil, that you may live. Then the Lord God Almighty will be with you, just as you say he is.

> Hate evil, love good; maintain justice in the courts. Perhaps the Lord God Almighty will have mercy (Amos 5:14–15).

God is looking at the unrighteousness of Britain and is judging us through the economy in such a way that we cannot resist his actions. He is the same God who judged Israel. Preceding the words of the prophets he sent other signs, including signs in unusual weather patterns, blight on crops, unusual sicknesses, shortage of food (recorded in Amos 4). There is also an unusual reference in chapter 1 and verse 1 to an earthquake which took place two years after Amos had prophesied to Israel. We should note this in relation to the prophecy concerning the first woe upon Britain, which is announced as a mighty earthquake which will swallow up the whole City. We can look back in our own nation to various signs in the weather, in health and in growing poverty.

When God judges a nation then people will suffer. He certainly warns the leaders of the nation and holds them responsible, but the nation as a whole can expect to suffer the consequences of its corporate sins. Judgement of the economy will have a major effect on the whole nation, as institutions in which we have put our confidence crumble. It will be as Amos said to Israel:

> 'There will be wailing in all the streets and cries of anguish in every public square. The farmers will be summoned to weep and the mourners to wail. There will be wailing in all the vineyards, for I will pass through your midst,' says the Lord. '. . . It will be as though a man fled from a lion only to meet a bear, as though he entered his house and rested his hand on the wall only to have a snake bite him' (Amos 5:16–17, 19).

The Lord is tired of striving with us and will not continue to protect us and bless us while we compromise truth and live dishonest lives, ignoring the Creator of the universe who has made it possible for us to become his children and live according to his ways. The words of Amos echo to us God's requirements for us in Britain as for the people of Israel in Amos' time: 'Let justice roll on like a river, righteousness like a never-failing stream!' (Amos 5:24). The accusation against our leaders is similar to that given by God to the leaders of Amos' day: 'Woe to you who are complacent in Zion, and to you who feel secure on Mount Samaria, you notable men of the foremost nation . . .' (6:1). Woe will indeed come when God declares judgement.

God's plumb line

Amos uses a number of symbols given to him in vision in order to make his message clear. In chapter 7 we see that God used the idea of a plumb line. This is a piece of string with a weight attached which is held up to a wall to check whether the wall is upright. God was setting a plumb line to the people of Israel to check how they measured up to his principles. He is doing the very same thing to Britain today. What is that plumb line? It is God's word. Israel did not heed the warning or measure up to the plumb line of God's word, and they lost everything when they were exiled from the land. Many people will lose everything when God shakes our nation through the economy. What things are being done in Britain today which are an abomination to God and are taking the nation out of the upright? Perhaps we should consider more carefully the plumb line that God has set up. It is by measuring ourselves by God's standards that the depth of our sin is exposed.

Exodus chapter 20 is a good starting point: the Ten Commandments given by God through Moses. Only a generation ago children were taught to recite the Ten Commandments from primary school on. Nowadays many have never read or heard them. They would not be able even to find the book of Exodus in the Bible. We would suggest that this is a measure of how far we have distanced ourselves from God's plumb line.

The Ten Commandments are only a beginning to understanding God's ways and walking close to him. There is much more to understand and it is time for our nation to humble itself and learn. Jesus taught:

> 'Love the Lord your God with all your heart and with all your soul and with all your mind.' This is the first and greatest commandment. And the second is like it: 'Love your neighbour as yourself.' All the Law and the Prophets hang on these two commandments (Matthew 22:37–40)

We can invent new laws for ourselves and try to live by them. Some of these laws, from the human point of view, may seem fair and reasonable. But if they are against the principles set out in the Bible, they are against God himself. We may not fully understand this, but we can understand the reality of the blessings that follow obedience or the curses that follow disobedience.

Britain is clearly 'out of plumb' at present and so it is time to seek God and discover what he requires us to do to be blessed. He will certainly carry out his judgements otherwise, and no one can say that the Bible was not available to be studied, that signs were not given, or that the prophets did not speak.

The message to Britain is to govern according to God's ways. For this to be effective we need strong national leaders who know and serve the living God. After this there is a deeper message to every individual, to believe in the Son of God, Jesus Christ, and to live in daily fellowship with God through Jesus Christ. There is not a covenant promise to the nation of Britain like there was to Israel, but there is one to the church, and there is a Coronation Oath which the Lord can use to bring us blessing if we return to the ways that this oath signifies.

Neither we nor Israel can love the Lord God with all our heart, soul and mind, or our neighbour as ourselves simply by changing the laws of the nation, but individuals who have a personal relationship with God through Jesus have a way open to true blessings in this life and an inheritance in the next life.

One might ask how a loving God can bring judgement on a nation. The answer lies in the fact that men and women bring this judgement on themselves. One of the judgements of God is to remove his hand of protection from a nation which is not obeying his laws. He knows full well what this will result in and his way of removing protection allows judgement to outwork itself just as he has determined. Herein is love, because he finds a way of judging godlessness, so that evil will be exposed, and so that people turn back to him. God can bring woes by direct action, as part of his judgements. He can also simply let evil run its course. One might ask how a loving God can allow suffering, but God surely asks how he can possibly go on protecting rebellious people who choose to do evil. If he does not remove his protection then men and women will mistake their evil for good, and things will go from bad to worse.

It is time for us to read the Bible and to consider if any of our ways offend the Lord. It is time for us to turn away from what is sinful and wicked and rebuild that which is good in God's eyes. If we consider the message of the prophets we will realise that God is sending us signs through nature and through the circumstances of our lives. Just as Amos could have been speaking directly to Britain, so could the prophet Haggai:

> Then the word of the Lord came through the prophet Haggai: 'Is it time for you yourselves to be living in your panelled houses, while this house remains a ruin?' Now this is what the Lord Almighty says: 'Give careful thought to your ways. You have planted much, but have harvested little. You eat, but never have enough. You drink, but never have your fill. You put on clothes but are not warm. You earn wages, only to put them in a purse with holes in it.' This is what the Lord Almighty says: 'Give careful thought to your ways! Go up into the mountains and bring down timber and build the house, so that I may take pleasure in it and be honoured,' says the Lord. 'You expected much, but see, it turned out to be little. What you brought home, I blew away. Why?' declares the Lord Almighty. 'Because of my house which remains a ruin, while each of you is busy with his own house. Therefore, because of you, the heavens have withheld their dew and the earth its crops. I called for a drought on the fields and the mountains, on the grain, the new wine, the oil and whatever the ground produces, on men and cattle, and on the labour of your hands' (Haggai 1:3–11).

When we read that last sentence the recent problems with BSE in Britain's cattle come to mind. This is surely a sign from God, but is just one among many other signs. When the blessings of our lives have been taken away it is time to turn back to God. This is the message of Haggai. There are signs in all of our lives that blessings have been removed, and that God is calling to us to build up this nation through his church, as he once called Israel to rebuild the temple.

Haggai also contains a promise that those who build according to God's pattern will be helped by him:

> 'But now be strong, O Zerubbabel,' declares the Lord. 'Be strong, O Joshua son of Jehozadak, the high priest. Be strong, all you people of the land,' declares the Lord, 'and work. For I am with you,' declares the Lord Almighty (Haggai 2:4).

The prophets of the Bible have a clear message for us today. It is time to seek God through faith in his Son Jesus Christ. He will help us to get our individual lives straight, if we turn to him, and he is also able to help us rebuild this nation. It is in love that he judges. When our economy collapses that will be an opportunity for us to come to our senses and rebuild in God's ways and with him, thanking him that he has not yet turned us completely over to the consequences of our sins. We will discover that it is the evil in the nation that is judged anyway, along with the institutions that are crushing the needy for whom God has compassion.

6

Earthquake in the City

> Hear, O earth: I am bringing disaster on this people, the fruit of their schemes, because they have not listened to my words and have rejected my law (Jeremiah 6:19).

The following prophecy announcing a mighty earthquake was given to Paul Slennett in February 1989. The alarm must be sounded all over Britain.

> My children, the alarm bells are sounding all over Europe, for judgement is being spoken out over the nations. Over your nation, Great Britain, a mighty earthquake is about to occur, an earthquake that will swallow up the whole City. Whole companies and city institutions will collapse in this earthquake, some never to rise again.
>
> My judgement that has been withheld for so long must now be unleashed on your nation in order that my church repent and lead this nation in repentance, for I am a Righteous and Holy God, just in all my ways, a God who longs to show mercy but one who will no longer tolerate the unrighteousness of my dear church. It is out of love that I visit this nation with judgement – you must know that this must always be the case. My children, repent now before it is too late, for already the day of my

return draws near and you must not be found wanting, like the virgins who did not fill their lamps with oil; but awake, my children, and be my watchmen, and speak with a prophetic voice of the judgement that is about to come upon the nations.

If you repent and turn from your wicked ways, I will visit your nation, Great Britain, once again, not with judgement, but with revival power, and I will protect you from all the strategy of the enemy.

In regard to Europe, come out of her, my dear children, for she will align herself with the Beast and the False Prophet who will arise and appear for just a short while. My children, take heart, for I am with you always. Do not give up, but pray without ceasing and see the salvation of your God.

We will use this chapter to review briefly the contents of the prophecy and to consider what it means. The issues raised in this chapter are also covered in greater detail throughout the book.

The opening sentence of the prophecy refers to the whole of Europe. If we try to interpret the signs of the times from God's perspective, we will see that Europe is moving into a situation which is not in accordance with his will. The gradual coming together of the Community of Nations in a political and economic union will not result in godliness in Europe, but quite the opposite. There will arise a religious framework to accompany the political and economic union, which will not be in God's will. Such a political, economic and religious framework is not what God wants. Through the prophecy and its timing he is reminding Britain of what it cost to hold on to her Reformation heritage, which she is about to give up in this false alliance, as well as losing her ability to govern herself as an autonomous sovereign nation. The warning covers the whole of Europe but, as we have seen, Britain has a particular standing with God.

The wording of the second sentence must be carefully weighed. There are both symbolic and practical aspects of the earthquake that is prophesied. The earthquake is 'over' the nation, which means that it is prophesied from heaven and will affect the whole nation. The words 'swallow up the whole City' imply that the whole financial structure which is called 'the City' will be affected in serious ways. We believe that a physical earthquake, wherever it strikes in the country, will be a part of the means by which a financial earthquake occurs. The prophecy says that 'whole companies and city institutions will collapse in this earthquake, some never to rise again'. The collapse of these companies and institutions could be interpreted as financial or physical or both. A physical earthquake would certainly cause physical damage and act as a sign of the coming financial collapse. It would also be a part of the means whereby the economic institutions are destabilised, accompanying other shock waves to the economy itself. Alongside any physical earthquake will be a shaking of the foundations upon which the economy is built. There will come a day of reckoning regarding excessive debt and unrighteous practice in the City, and in such a day some financial institutions and companies will become bankrupt, taking with them the savings and employment of ordinary people. Some of these institutions and companies will disappear from the financial market-place for ever. It could be that a physical earthquake will strike at the heart of at least one part of our economy which displeases God most and represents the nation's pride and independence from God: for example, the channel tunnel. If the earthquake did occur here, this would cut the physical link with Europe, confirming God's displeasure at this alliance. It would destabilise the banks that have invested heavily in the tunnel project, and confirm the island status of Britain. An earthquake in the southeast of England could also shake the City of London itself; some companies and institutions could shake physically or even collapse, coinciding with the financial collapse. We must not discount this possibility.

When this earthquake comes, it will be dramatic and sudden, maybe at a time when the economy seems to be climbing. This is often a pattern of God's judgements:

> While people are saying, 'Peace and safety,' destruction will come on them suddenly, as labour pains on a pregnant woman, and they will not escape (1 Thess 5:3).

We must realise, however, that it is not just the economy of Britain that is under judgement, it is all the sinful ways of the nation that God is addressing. He is striking at the economy in order to bring a woe to the whole nation so that we will repent of our sins and turn to him. The economy, rather than God's word, has become the foundation of our nation, but when that foundation is shaken, we can rebuild true foundations again.

We note that the prophecy is to the church in particular. Let's consider just what that means. The Church of England still represents the nation in many ways, and God may be addressing more people than we might think. Many claim to be Anglican but never go to church. Many claim to be believers but live in sin, such as adultery or homosexual relationships. God may be addressing the backsliders too when he addresses his church today. It may not be too late to repent and turn the national church back to him, even though it is desperately lukewarm and sinful. But the opportunity may not last for much longer.

The word 'repentance' means turning away from something sinful and turning towards God and his ways. It involves recognition and confession of sin (which is wrongdoing, or falling short of God's standards) and turning to him in prayer, resolving to learn to do what is right, and cease to do what is wrong. We may fulfil God's standards in some areas of life but not in others, and it is the sinful areas of our lives that he wants us to put right. The church should know God's ways. This is why judgement comes to the church first. Then the church will be in a position to lead others to understand the ways of God and to repentance.

Holiness means being separate from all that is sinful. God is holy, but he is also patient. The prophecy shows that his patience with Britain has been stretched to the limit. He cannot continue to bless those who are sinking further and further into sinful ways. Yet his action in bringing an economic woe (a painful set of circumstances coming into our lives, while blessings are withheld) is not to harm us, but to bring us to repentance. There is a principle embedded in the teaching of the Bible that shows that God treats us like children when he brings punishments to us for our own good. It is better to be treated like this than for God to abandon us altogether.

> Endure hardship as discipline; God is treating you as sons. For what son is not disciplined by his father? If you are not disciplined (and everyone undergoes discipline), then you are illegitimate children and not true sons.

> Moreover, we have all had human fathers who disciplined us and we respected them for it. How much more should we submit to the Father of our spirits and live! Our fathers disciplined us for a little while as they thought best; but God disciplines us for our good that we may share in his holiness. No discipline seems pleasant at the time, but painful. Later on, however, it produces a harvest of righteousness and peace for those who have been trained by it (Hebrews 12:7–11).

These verses explain much of the second paragraph of the prophecy.

The virgins who did not fill their lamps with oil is a reference to the parable in Matthew 25. This story warns us to be ready for the return of the Lord Jesus. He is coming back to this earth, and he will judge all who have ever lived on the face of the earth. The time for Jesus' return is drawing near. God's judgements are coming and he is giving us time to prepare.

From the third paragraph of the prophecy we understand that God is willing to bring protection to this nation once more. 'Revival' means waking up or bringing back to life. God has ways of waking us up and refreshing us spiritually, sending conviction of sin and forgiveness. There have been many spiritual revivals in Britain and they have come with such power that whole communities have been turned to God and his ways, as well as men being moved to turn the nation's law and social structures into a godly framework. As a result of the Welsh revival, beginning in 1904, many Christian missionaries were sent out of Britain to the whole world. At times of spiritual revival God delivers people from sinfulness into new life in Jesus and gives them new vision and hope.

The book of Revelation makes it clear that there

will come a time on this earth when a totally ungodly authority will take over for a short while. This will be so horrific that it will be classed as 'the Beast'. As well as a spiritual power over the whole earth, the Beast refers to a person who manifests this power as a world leader, and is also known as the Antichrist, putting himself in the place of Jesus Christ. The 'False Prophet' is the one who will claim to speak truth but will mislead people into following this Beast. We have seen what can happen in Europe through the rise of Naziism. A man who is totally taken over by Satan can rise to power and bewitch or trap a nation into following him. The result can be at least as horrific as the Second World War. If such a system can rise once it can rise again.

There are those who can already see the similarities between the plans that Hitler had for Europe and today's European Union. In their book, *Treason at Maastricht*, Rodney Atkinson and Norris McWhirter list ten significant parallels between the two plans for Europe, including common policies on basic commodities, a common currency and banking systems, a common labour policy, the single market, and works councils. Such a rule could come to the European Community, once there is a firm alliance, that is as evil as we saw in Germany in the war years. It may not be the same in character. It may be more seductive. But there will arise rulers who are in Satan's hands and whose only goal is world domination. They will trap the world into a political, economic and religious system which will mean bondage of many kinds in the lives of ordinary people, and the persecution of true followers of Jesus Christ. The Beast will have one supreme motive, and that will be to destroy true faith on the earth and to cause people to follow him instead of the one true and living God. He will so bind up economic systems that no one will be able to buy or sell without the mark of the Beast on their forehead or hand. This could easily come about with computer technology, and very soon, though the real mark will be a spiritual allegiance to Satan through worship of the Beast. Then there will be no turning back, but only banishment to hell at Judgement Day. A world government and a one-world economy may encompass a new spirituality, allied with the New Age Movement, which itself is a blend of Eastern mystery religions, including Hinduism, Taoism and Buddhism. Even witchcraft and satanism are doorways into the New Age Movement. The 'enemy' spoken about in the prophecy is Satan and his fallen angels and all who follow him.

Britain has been protected from false religions until this generation. It has been able to maintain Protestant Christianity against all pressures. It has withstood Communism and Naziism. We are being warned that the European Union will become a snare to us and bring us into a situation of defeat that is subtly wrought, eroding all that for which we once stood firm. We are warned to come out of this alliance. The economic shaking that God will give us may be the best means to break the present dishonest system, but it could also be the means of our being ejected from Europe. We are to pray for this. We are not to give up when the pressure comes, but to seek God who will help us.

We have all been in families and some of us have our own children. We know the agony of parenthood when our children fail to come up to expectations despite all our love and our efforts. We know the pain we suffer in inflicting punishment, or watching our children suffer from their own mistakes. God in heaven is also the Father of his own family on earth, and he agonises over his children much more than any human father. He suffers with us as he brings his judgements, but he knows they are necessary. He is more patient than any earthly father, but he cannot compromise.

We remember finally the sentence that was inserted in Paul Slennett's letter at the time of the postmark: 'Woe! Woe! Woe! to this nation if it refuses to accept his proclamation that "Jesus is Alive!" and that he died on the cross for our sins that we might be forgiven.'

What else can God do, now that the price has been paid for our sins, other than ask us to accept the free gift through repentance and belief? What else can he do other than let us reap what we sow in our own lives if we reject this gift? What else can he do other than send warnings and unsettle us so that we will realise that we have chosen ungodly ways? Yet as he pronounces each of those woes, he tears his heart and suffers with us – because he loves us.

7

Judgement Across the Nations

> This sin will become for you like a high wall, cracked and bulging, that collapses suddenly, in an instant (Isaiah 30:13).

The economy of the whole world is unstable and ready for collapse. In the light of what we know of God's ways, let us look at some of the signs of the times around the world.

The English hurricane

During the day of Thursday 15th October 1987 weather forecasters had no idea of the intensity of the hurricane that would hit Britain later that night. There was no warning from the meteorology stations, and the weather patterns predicted only winds up to 30 mph with gusts up to 50 mph – quite a normal sort of forecast for the time of year. In fact an anonymous caller telephoned the BBC during the day to warn them that a hurricane was coming. This was treated so lightly that, in the weather forecast on television that evening, the presenter, Michael Fish, even joked about it.

During that evening, on ITV's 10.30 pm *City Programme*, a City fund manager was asked about the use of modern computing techniques, such as 'program trading', which sell more as the market falls according to a sophisticated mathematical formula. He was asked whether the increasing dependence on advanced computer techniques could cause a major market crash. Even as he said confidently that such dependence could not, of itself, cause it, the wind was beginning to whistle around the City's office blocks.

A low pressure developed in a way that our most sophisticated instruments did not predict, and the hurricane hit the South East of England with an intensity never before recorded. By the grace of God, the hurricane struck at night and so the damage to human life was minimised (eighteen people lost their lives). Yet hundreds of millions of pounds' worth of damage occurred. Millions of trees were torn up, many of which brought power lines down. The homes of some people were severely damaged. Bob Ogley and Kev Adams published photographs and gave graphic accounts of what happened that night, in their best-selling book *Eye of the Hurricane*. They wrote in the Introduction:

> In the early hours of the morning forests were destroyed, aircraft overturned, lorries blown over, cars crushed and roofs and walls sucked from houses and churches. In every community from the Thames to the Wash life came to a standstill.

In their chapter, 'The Most Expensive Night Ever', they describe the tens of thousands of insurance claims that followed and the '100,000 disturbed and shattered lives' of people in the immediate aftermath of the hurricane. The British Government was put into a condition of alarm after the 110 mph hurricane had torn into an area of the country where, coincidentally, many of the more wealthy of society live, leaving a trail of extreme damage.

Next morning, some City traders and fund managers found that they could not leave their houses because trees blocked their drive-ways. Others set off by train from the North West of London, ignorant of the situation in the South East. The trains did not make it – one fund manager's train hit a tree north of Watford Junction, limped into the station and terminated, so he had to call his wife to be rescued. In office blocks rain and winds had broken windows, damaged computers and disrupted the critical communication conduits. There were no back-up contingency plans, unlike the aftermath of the Bishopsgate bomb when the City was back to work within forty-eight hours. As well as the financial loss from the hurricane's damage, the Stock Exchange, the Bank of England and the entire City of London were out of action for the whole of Friday 16th October.

The economic storm

The vulnerability of the world trading system is demonstrated at times like this. Trading is run on tight schedules of buying and selling. Computers and telephone lines in the City of London and in other financial capitals are caught up in a tight web of buying and selling where seconds can make the difference between profit or loss. Any disruption to this trading can have devastating effects.

However, trading *did* occur in New York. Hard on the heels of a correction downwards on the Thursday, a further move downwards in the last hours of trading on Friday 16th left the world markets vulnerable. Japan was nervous, with trading opening down in the very early hours of the following Monday morning. UK traders and managers tried to make it into work early on the Monday morning, being aware of the recent severe falls around the world, but were frustrated by continuing problems due to storm damage. Worse still, they could not communicate with their offices.

Those who did make it in were greeted by computers which did not work, offices with no phones or power, and sodden printed records. They were confronted with the Japanese market falling, and the US market having fallen significantly for two trading days without London having been open since the previous Thursday. Often, it was the younger and less experienced traders or managers, who still lived in London, who made it into the office first. The boss had enjoyed the 'golden days' of the mid-80s to line his pockets and purchase the ultimate 'des. res.' in the 'stockbroker belt'. The only conclusion – in the absence of information, experience, or access to your boss – was sell! The London market went into free fall, and New York followed suit when it opened at 1.30 pm London time. The weak New York opening precipitated further falls in London. By the end of that day in New York, a far steeper decline in US share values had occurred than in the crash of 1929, taking one quarter of the value from shares.

This illustrates how the vulnerable stock markets across the world can suddenly collapse together when uncertainty spreads and trading is affected. The physical hurricane was a clear sign from God, and a warning. Behind the scenes were rising debts and a trading system very susceptible to either 'hurricanes' or 'earthquakes'. The best brains in the world are employed in the financial institutions, and the most sophisticated modern equipment. Trading across the world is carried out with rapid communications facilities and the latest techniques of economics. Yet hurricanes and earthquakes of both physical and economic kinds can bring collapse within hours, defying the best systems that mankind can produce. Surely the evidence shows that God has power, beyond the wit of man, to judge these systems. If there is unrighteousness then the day of reckoning will come.

In his book, *Sound the Trumpet among the Nations* (published in 1991 by Christian Foundation Publications), the Revd David Gardner records that his Bible reading for that very morning was, 'Shall there be evil in a city, and the Lord hath not done it?' (Amos 3:6). At an address given to the Foreign Office Christian Union on the following 16th February, David reminded his audience that only hours before the hurricane, at the end of the Conservative Party Conference, Prime Minister Margaret Thatcher had declared, 'We have made Britain strong once again. We are strong economically, strong industrially, strong technologically. We have brought about a revival!' David challenged his audience:

> This is what was proudly declared. God was not acknowledged in any way. *We* had done all this! You must never say that – would somebody please tell her! And God just said 'Phooph'. He blew with His winds! A *Daily Telegraph* leader the very next morning said: 'In John

Milton's day – that hurricane would have been attributed to God expressing His immense displeasure at Britain.' I should think so! But I would remind you that the God of John Milton's day is the same God today. I would also remind you that King Nebuchadnezzar, in the prophet Daniel's day, proudly proclaimed from the roof of his palace, 'Is not this the great Babylon, that I have built . . .?' While the word was in the king's mouth, there fell a voice from heaven saying, 'The Kingdom is departed from thee' (Daniel 4:30–31). And it happened! And the same thing could happen today.

Eastern Europe

In Europe the alarm bells of unusual weather patterns have already been mentioned. There is also the sign of the dramatic and unexpected collapse of Communism which affected all the countries of Eastern Europe. The collapse of Communism and the tearing down of the Berlin Wall was at the end of 1989.

President Gorbachev's new thinking led to the lifting of restrictions which had prevented Jews from leaving Russia. This was a sign of a new openness which was developing. By 1987, the Soviet role in Afghanistan ceased. They had fought to maintain a Communist government in Afghanistan since the late 1970s, a confrontation between Communism and Islam which also produced tension between the Soviets and other leading nations. Now, this tension was eased. In Poland the independent labour movement called Solidarity, once outlawed, deposed the Communist government in early 1989 and became the first non-Communist government in Eastern Europe since the late 1940s.

The Berlin Wall came down on 9th November 1989.

People celebrated and danced on top of the wall just before it was brought down by the bulldozers – activity which would previously have led to instant death.

Between November and late December 1989 the five Communist governments of Hungary, East Germany, Bulgaria, Czechoslovakia and Romania were all replaced by non-Communist governments, all of which moved towards establishing multi-party democratic systems and market economies.

In June 1991, the largest democratic election in Soviet history was held in Russia, and by the end of the year the whole Communist Bloc had broken up and was being reorganised into a new Commonwealth of Independent States. Such was the rapidity of the changes that came to Eastern Europe.

Britain

For three centuries, Lloyds of London developed a reputation for integrity and fair trading, but towards the end of the 1980s disaster struck, destroying that reputation. It meant financial crisis for the list of 'Names'. These are people who underwrite business transactions within the syndicates into which the company is divided. From the point of view of these investors, the pledge of money is relatively safe and will lead to profits from the transactions carried out by Lloyds. However, should there be a sudden financial problem, the money which was pledged would be called in. During the 1980s two things happened in Lloyds. First, there was a move to recruit more 'Names', and the small number of underwriters was greatly increased through the addition of many people who wanted both to acquire the status of being a 'Name' and gather some of the 'easy' profits. Thus, at the backbone of Lloyds of London by the late 1980s were thousands of new members of moderate means. Secondly, there was an internal spiral of reinsuring. This is a process by which those who underwrite certain sums with some syndicates then take out insurance policies with other syndicates to minimise any sudden loss that the market brings.

An enormous set of insurance claims came in from asbestos related policies in America. The assumption had been that these cases would take many years to settle in the American courts, but suddenly, settlements were being made and judges began to award huge damages to industrial workers. Liabilities at Lloyds threatened to exceed the reserves of the syndicates. Claims then began to come in from the Piper Alpha oil platform catastrophe in July 1988, followed by Hurricane Hugo and the Exxon Valdez disaster. Suddenly Lloyds was facing losses of billions of pounds and Names were called upon to pay what they had pledged. Many, particularly among the newcomers to Lloyds, faced ruin.

On 5th November 1991, Robert Maxwell was reported drowned at sea, having disappeared overboard from his private yacht. Shortly afterwards the whole publishing empire was seen to be collapsing. Maxwell had got into financial difficulties and fraudulently taken about half a billion pounds from the pension fund of his relatively stable Mirror Group Newspapers. This sudden exposure was followed by complex court cases, while 32,000 past and present employees were robbed of their savings.

The late 1980s and early 1990s saw other major companies collapse in different ways. In 1990

Coloroll, the wallpaper and fabrics manufacturers, collapsed with debts of £400 million. Polly Peck International, the fruit packaging and electrical goods company, crashed with £1.3 billion debts. In 1992, Mountleigh, a company dealing with commercial property, collapsed with debts of £590 million. These were big organisations, but it is also reported that during 1992, on average, one small company went bankrupt every minute and a half.

Meanwhile, in Europe, these and other instabilities at government level led to a constant strain on attempts to develop the Exchange Rate Mechanism (ERM) in Europe. It was beyond the ability of Britain's Chancellor of the Exchequer to use the methods at his disposal to keep the British economy stable enough to remain in the European mechanism. This is another clue to a vulnerable economy which can quickly go out of control. There are times when it is clearly shown that the best brains and the best machines and methods in the world – from a human viewpoint – are inadequate to the task of keeping the world economy stable.

All these things do not add up to a financial earthquake. They are warning tremors at the most. A mighty earthquake will disturb the whole foundation of the economy and come in a surprising and sudden way. Nevertheless, these situations give us some clues to instability and alert us to the fact that a financial collapse could indeed happen suddenly.

The 1987 financial problems, including the effects of the physical hurricane, showed that the economies of many countries in the world are interwoven. What happens in one country can have a major effect on what happens in another.

The American debt

Looking across the world, we see that, in America, national debt is a seemingly insurmountable problem. In February of 1996 the debt was admitted to be around five thousand billion dollars. Even this figure is seen as under-estimating the problem when such national funds as Social Security are considered in addition. Since 1994 the debt has been more than 70% of the nation's annual income (GDP). One day the annual interest could be higher than the whole income and then the nation will be bankrupt. Though America recovered from the 1987 stock-market difficulties, a total collapse of the economy could come about. This would be followed, like a shock wave, by financial problems across the world, leading to another great depression, as in the 1930s. One sequence of events that could happen in America is a period of declining productivity, caused by very rapid inflation, followed by bankruptcy – a forecast made by some economists today.

In an unstable world economy America will be vulnerable due to the large foreign ownership of US Treasury Bonds. If a situation arises where there is panic selling of these bonds in any one of several countries, this could send a shock wave through the American economy. In 1996 foreign governments and overseas investors held almost one thousand billion dollars' worth of America's national debt in bonds, including $255 billion in Japan, $142 billion in Britain, $64 billion in Germany and $34 billion in China. America could soon find itself in the situation of Proverbs 22:7, where 'the rich rule over the poor and the borrower is servant to the lender'.

America is receiving other warnings, however. For example, the earthquake in San Francisco, which occurred during October 1989 and was the costliest natural disaster in the history of America (approximately $12 billion worth of damage) is one such sign. One of the after-shocks of such a disaster is felt by insurers. The biggest insurer of property affected by the 1989 disaster was Lloyds of London. Another earthquake in Los Angeles, on 17th January 1994, had its epicentre right under the main headquarters of the pornography industry of America. This earthquake was not classed as 'the Big One', which is still to come, according to the scientists who monitor earthquakes, but surely there are warning signs of judgement from God when right at the centre of the earthquake were seventy companies which produced 95% of the pornographic videos made each year in the United States, an industry with an annual revenue of $3 billion.

The Far East

Japan is another economy which has seemed strong, but has suddenly weakened over the last couple of years. Some of the weakening has come at a time when corruption is also being exposed, such as when it was revealed that a bank executive in Daiwa Bank was discovered to have lost $1.1 billion, related to unpaid bills in the USA over the decade up to 1995. The whole Japanese economy has been affected by bad loans of an estimated $1.2 thousand million. The confidence in trading with Japan has deteriorated so that the Stock Market has had sudden falls.

It is interesting that the difficulties with the

Japanese economy have also been accompanied by a major earthquake. This was in Kobe in January 1995. The direct losses due to the earthquake and resulting fires amounted to billions of dollars and there have been ongoing repercussions for the nation and for overseas companies linked through trade. A headline in *The Times* of 31st August 1995 read, 'Kobe after-shock hits Japan's precarious financial system'. The opening paragraph read, 'The devastating earthquake in Kobe last January shook Japan's economy and financial markets almost as violently as the people in that city. It exposed the madness of dealings on the Nikkei stock index by Nick Leeson which brought down Barings. When the Nikkei looked as if it might be bottoming out, the earthquake sent the index on another disastrous downward leg.'

Barings Bank was among the most respected of British institutions for many years but it was destroyed by one young executive, Nick Leeson, who was trading speculatively and beyond his means.

The last big earthquake to hit Tokyo was in 1923. This was larger than the Kobe earthquake, and wiped out wealth equivalent to one third of the gross domestic product of the time. Most of the property damage was by resulting fires. There were 100,000 deaths and two thirds of all homes were destroyed. Despite the improvement in earthquake precautions, if the 1995 earthquake had hit Tokyo instead of Kobe, the resulting damage to buildings would have amounted to $30 billion in central Tokyo alone. This, in turn, would have led to insurance claims, which would have impacted London, where a large proportion of the reinsurance has been placed. Lloyd's of London is responsible for much of this. It is estimated, by the widely accepted Kawasumi theory, that an earthquake of this nature can be expected on average every sixty-nine years. Therefore, Tokyo can expect a major earthquake any day, which would send shock waves through the world's economies.

Trading standards

Economists across the world know just how vulnerable we are at present and many are expecting some form of major catastrophe. This is shown by the growing number of books on economics that are in the shops, which highlight the growing uncertainties of the world's economies. Economists know that there are some areas more vulnerable than others, such as the derivatives markets. It is beyond the ability of most of us to understand the complex way these markets work. Only those who work in the systems know the details.

In the case of derivatives, a US commission made a recent study and presented the facts. Derivatives are run on a market system separate from the Stock and Bond Markets and the Foreign Exchange Markets, but linked with them. They represent an enormous and growing aspect of trading. Apparently, in the first half of the 1990s the derivative financial markets accounted for around $50 thousand million. One example of the derivative market is where risks are covered by finding alternative buyers as insurance against wrong predictions. A buyer may set up a purchase based on his view that there will be a price increase in the commodity. This may be on the basis of foreign exchange values changing, for example. As an insurance, he will arrange for a second party, who believes the market will decrease in value rather than increase, to purchase the option (technically termed 'writing a put') on this commodity. A third party, the broker, sets up the deal between these two parties at a commission. As the market forces then move, profits are taken by either side. Other ways of covering risks are also implemented which take account of fluctuating currency values and others relate to buying and selling across international boundaries, where different factors have to be taken into account. Economists are concerned that there will come a day of reckoning when the web of schemes relating to derivatives simply collapses. On such a day, the instability and unrighteousness of the systems will be revealed. Many will face the consequences of debts being called in.

Economies today incorporate many such schemes, worked out by experts with modern technology at their fingertips and a knowledge of the way others trade. There are devices such as programmed buying, where transactions are set up to take effect automatically when currency exchange rates or profit margins hit the required level. There are methods of forward buying, so that sales are delayed until profit margins accumulate. This is done by wealthy speculators, including banks. There are also 'hedge funds', which are highly speculative ventures where secretive groups trade on large amounts of borrowed money. Then there are the intricate webs of securities built in through insurance and other means so that losses are minimised should there be miscalculations of how the markets will move. These are not illegal methods of trading, but they involve much risk-taking. Indeed, it is suggested that there is no success in career terms in the City if one is not a high risk-taker.

Economists know that the whole world market-place could collapse suddenly, but no one is capable of back-tracking to simpler methods of trading now that the machinery of world trading simply keeps moving.

However, it is also anticipated that it is possible to recover from economic collapse. Some businesses will go down maybe, but others will weather the storm. Of course, this is open to conjecture, but it is likely that economies can be built again on the same or similar principles when instability leads to collapse of some sectors. The decline or loss of some institutions and companies is a problem for some, but others will grow to fill the gaps created in the market-place.

So we can see that it will take something more than an unstable and internally collapsing economy to make us realise that God is speaking. Something will have to happen which economists *cannot* predict or from which they cannot plan recovery; something that will have strong evidence of the intervention of Almighty God. Thus a physical earthquake, particularly one which takes us by surprise, is not an unreasonable thing to expect as a judgement from God, causing us to rethink the principles of our economy.

It is important to note that, despite the strength that economic bases like Tokyo and New York have had, London is still reckoned to be the major centre of world finance, and the square mile of the City of London is the most concentrated area of financial activity on the planet. If some of the City's institutions were shaken physically or economically or both, in a way that they could not recover, the after-effect would be like a shock wave going out to the whole world.

Though the trading techniques in the modern world are not considered illegal in the world's terms, they are far from the principles of the Bible. The market-place of the world is concerned more about profits than it is about service. The principles of not lending for gain, care of the poor, serving the community, using equal scales and fair weights – these have been lost in a web of intricate manoeuvring for personal gain. Commodities are bought and sold to further the productivity and serve the needs of the modern world, of course, but at the heart of our business is the desire to make gains at the expense of others and with as little risk as possible. We are all caught up in this 'get-rich-quick' society either because that is our desire or because that is the principle on which our savings are invested. When the banks or other investment corporations collapse, so will the investments of many ordinary people who do not have a say in the day-to-day running of the Stock Markets.

When Jesus overturned the tables of the traders in the Temple, many of them probably thought that they were doing justified trading, but their standards had slipped from God's ways. So it is with us. God may be about to turn our tables over. When he does, we will realise just how far our lives have been interwoven with the economy of the country. It will hurt, in ways that we may not have realised, but what better way is there for bringing us back to our senses? We will be in a position to realise that a vulnerable economy, like a bulging wall, has been pushed over by God.

Debt in Britain

Within Britain personal debt is rising. In June 1996 there were 30 million credit cards, and spending on these cards is climbing at a steady rate. Estimates of

£10 billion debt on the two most popular cards alone have been given, with an annual growth rate of 10%. Government borrowing in Britain is estimated to be around £27 billion for 1996 alone. At the beginning of the century this nation was debt free. Now debt is rising at government level and personal level at alarming rates. Like the banks our stability can collapse when the debts are called in.

When an economic collapse occurs, there will be shock waves through the lives of every person, particularly those in debt, or living beyond their means – the unemployed, those with mortgages higher than they can afford, students on grants who have taken out loans. Many of these are the most vulnerable in society and debt could lead to housing repossessions, inability to pay rents, no money for food to eat, or for health-care, when other debts have to be paid. Some will lose their investments through insurance related mortgages at the end of their term, where the accumulated funds will have become insufficient to pay off the mortgage. It is not always those who have sinned most who most feel the effects of a collapsing system, but we can all take some steps to untangle ourselves before the collapse occurs. We can turn to an infinitely loving God when things go wrong. He understands the web of bondage that we are in through our sins, some of them economic, but there is a remedy for sin, and the price was paid on the cross at Calvary.

Earthquakes in Britain

When the earthquake in the City strikes, it must be seen as the act of a loving, patient and holy God as well as of an uncompromising judge. God has righteousness and love in perfect balance. Those who find a path of repentance will discover a loving Father. There is no doubt about that. Those who seek God with all their heart will certainly find him, and when they do, they will realise that it was their own errors which led them away from him. They will find complete forgiveness through repentance and faith, and a fresh start, with God himself to help with the rebuilding of life.

There have been some deaths from earthquakes in Britain, though they are not as common as in many other countries. In 1580, two people died in London when an earthquake struck along a fault line from Kent to Belgium. In 1884, 1,200 homes were flattened and four people were killed by an earthquake in Colchester, Essex. More recently, in 1984, an earthquake, recording 5.4 on the Richter scale, struck North Wales, and shocks were felt all round the country. Then in 1990 a twenty-second tremor at Wrexham, in the same area of North Wales, measuring 5.2 on the Richter scale, toppled chimneys and caused other structural damage. Houses right across to the Midlands had to be evacuated as the shocks were felt.

The *Sunday Times* of 15th September 1996 carried the headline, 'London could face quake of LA scale, say geologists'. This referred to a report from the British Geological Survey, which highlighted the fact that a major earthquake occurs at roughly 200-year intervals in the southeast of England, due to a fault running under the Dover Straits. Earthquakes of 1382, 1580 and 1776 rocked both London and the southeast. If stress is continuing to build up in this area it may result in an even larger earthquake in the near future. The channel tunnel, which many people believe was not built according to God's purposes for Britain, has incurred huge losses and is built near this fault line.

An earthquake is a sudden movement of the ground due to the release of stresses in the rocks of the earth, along lines of weakness called faults. The most intense earthquake would have a rating of about 9 on the Richter scale. The highest recorded earthquake in Britain was on the 7th June 1931 at Dogger Bank, measuring up to 6.1 on the Richter scale. Britain has about 360 minor earthquakes each year of which around thirty are felt, but are not usually damaging. There are no reliable scientific ways of forecasting earthquakes at present. When an earthquake strikes, it is better not to be in the vicinity, of course, but if one is caught up in it, the best action, according to the UK Earthquake Monitoring Service, is to 'move carefully to an open area, away from buildings and power lines, as soon as it is safe to do so'. We can apply the same principle to financial difficulties, or to sin of any kind.

When God brings the shaking to the nation which will be accompanied by a physical earthquake, it will be better to be free of the bondages associated with debt and improper business dealings. Such an earthquake could come when many people are caught in the periods between buying and selling – when they are most vulnerable. At such a time those who have speculated with other people's money or invested beyond their own ability to pay will be found out. God can provide a way out for those who truly seek him, but we must also face up, at that time, to the consequences of the sins of the nation and of our own lives, whether they are financial or of other kinds.

8

Consequences of the Financial Collapse

> Therefore everyone who hears these words of mine and puts them into practice is like a wise man who built his house on the rock. The rain came down, the streams rose, and the winds blew and beat against that house; yet it did not fall, because it had its foundation on the rock (Matthew 7:24–25).

Some economists are themselves predicting a financial crisis in the near future. By studying economic trends, business cycles can be identified, making it possible to predict what will come next. There is a cycle which comes round every nine to eleven years. A period of prosperity is followed by a crisis, then by liquidation of assets and then by a recession. Economists would not be surprised to hear us predicting financial trouble ahead within these known economic cycles.

Inevitably, it is the calling in of debts that causes liquidation of assets, which in turn leads to companies closing, bankruptcy and personal hardship. Sometimes the cycle involves inflation, followed by liquidation, followed by depression. It is the responsibility of those in leadership positions to guide the nation safely through the economic cycles, avoiding potential troubles, but peaks and troughs in the economic systems of the world are to be expected.

Is there a difference then between what we are saying in this book and what economists already know? The answer is that the coming economic earthquake will be a judgement from God. God will produce something which is partly understood by economists, but not totally predictable. God will bring about a situation that could not be foreseen by any economist – an economic collapse linked to an earthquake in Britain. It will come suddenly, and may even be at a time when there are positive signs in the economy. It will come in such a way that economic strategies will not be able to prevent the consequences that follow. We will be in a situation which prompts us to rethink the foundations of both our economy and our society. We are about to feel what an economic earthquake is like. It could resemble the devastation following a world war. It could be as severe as anything in our history, including the fire of London in 1666.

In the Great Depression of the 1930s, there were two main factors that made the economy vulnerable. These were speculation and debt – the two factors at the background of our own troubled economy today.

Speculation at the lowest level could be called gambling. It involves trying to make gains by taking risks with investments. That can mean anything from betting on horses or playing the National Lottery to high level investing on the Stock Market, or in the spirals of insurance and reinsurance of the financial institutions, and in the derivative market. It reflects a 'get-rich-quick' society. But it is impossible for everyone to get rich and so some become casualties of the system at the expense of others. The worst result of speculation is the mentality it fosters. It is not easily married with contentment in working honestly and steadily for a fair wage. Rather, there grows a desire for personal prestige or survival at the expense of others, with no desire to serve the community. Speculation can also mean being tempted to live beyond one's means. When we do this there is a major collapse in our lifestyle when we can no longer live on borrowed money. This is what we will have to face when the economic system is shaken.

Debt is the other issue. At a time of financial collapse, debts will be called in and that will hit the individuals who must pay up, or the companies that have to sell off their assets. We have seen how debt is a major problem at both national and personal levels. On average, during the early part of the 1990s, people in Britain had debts equal to just over 100% of their annual income. The time is coming when those debts will have to be paid.

Many of us have come to depend on luxury items such as washing machines, vacuum cleaners, cars and televisions. Even those at the lower end of the income bracket, and even those living on Social Security, have a range of modern electrical equipment to ease the burdens of life. We have not known food shortages for many years. We have been able to have heat and light at the flick of a switch. Clean water is readily available and our waste disposal has been efficient. We have been able to communicate with one another through letters or telephone. We have an efficient service for emergencies, such as fire or sudden sickness. An education system is available for all our children. We have had the best of healthcare. Our law enforcement has been largely successful, and we have been safe from military invasion.

However, in many of the important service areas, including schools, hospitals and social welfare, there are signs of increasing pressure and, despite all our benefits, there is growing discontent and lawlessness. These are initial signs of how such services might collapse and discontent might arise should a crisis suddenly come.

Learning from the past

The consequences of the coming financial collapse depend on its severity and how we respond. It is going to be severe, and there are worrying signs in our society that we could go into a time of anarchy and chaos, rather than co-operation and rebuilding. But there are many lessons from the history of Britain showing that it is possible to rebuild in co-operation, putting up with hardship rather than sinking into despair. Such days of co-operation do bring a certain blessing, when we are brought together in a special way, learning to appreciate what we have and what each person can do for the good of others.

In the past, this country has known massive unemployment, when even skilled people couldn't find work, and social service benefits were not so readily available. We have known food shortages, when charitable soup-kitchens have been opened to feed the hungry. But can we imagine now the loss of basic services such as electricity or rubbish disposal? Can we imagine streets filling with uncollected refuse and attracting vermin to our homes? Can we imagine what it will be like when we have to queue for limited supplies of food and cannot readily have a doctor's appointment for our sicknesses? Can we imagine what it will be like when our schools close for lack of funds, or teachers, or heating.

When the nation was thrown into the Second World War, we faced the challenge together and came through, and after the war, communities were rebuilt. Yes, there was rationing of food, and fewer luxuries, but out of the circumstances we built the best education system in the world, the best social stuctures for the care of the infirm, elderly and handicapped. Family life was a focal point. Healthy outdoor activities for the young were part of their education, without the massive-scale temptations of drugs and pornography we have today. Practical trades were valued and we had training programmes to equip our work force for the tasks ahead. The Sabbath day was kept holy, as quiet descended upon the nation each Sunday. We could do all this again. This time we must be careful not to be too ambitious, too selfish.

What will it be like?

Each of us can look at the present condition of Britain and our own circumstances and imagine what the results of a financial collapse could bring to our lives. The bleak picture can be terrifying.

After many years of affluence it is hard for many of us to imagine what the nation will be like following a disaster. This is particularly true of the younger generation who have only known the last two or three decades. Older people know what it is to have survived a world war and to have rebuilt the nation. Some can recall the Depression of the 1930s. They are likely to have a more mature view of the crisis, provided they have not come to expect affluence as a right for which they have fought.

From the Depression of the 1930s we can learn about economic hardship. When the value of money suddenly changes, people become unclear about how they will be able to afford to live day by day even in relation to their simple needs for food, clothing, health-care and housing. Suddenly everything becomes uncertain and there is no easy way out any more. It is not possible to live on credit and the money coming in barely pays the bills.

People tend to withdraw their money from banks at times when the economy shakes. This worsens the situation of some banks, who can no longer trade and so go into liquidation. Also, during these times of uncertainty, those who provide basic essentials, such as food from the farms, are not confident to sell because of fluctuation in values and prices. This leads to shortages and unpredictability. When industries are not trading smoothly, there follow lay-offs of employees, and the collapse of even essential industries can follow. After the 1930s, for example, the industries of coal, cotton, steel and shipbuilding were permanently weakened, despite the fact that world markets for these commodities recovered.

Suddenly there is no credit to be had and existing debts have to be paid. People have to sell what they have in order to pay debts. Companies have to sell off their assets. Bankruptcies follow. The value of assets decreases as there is panic selling to pay debts. Every sort of commodity is suddenly on the market – homes, art treasures, cars, household effects and so on, but not necessarily attracting buyers, even at very low selling prices.

Then follows unemployment and people wonder if they have value or purpose in life. They find it impossible to maintain the lifestyle that they once had and now they wonder if they have any value to society at all. They can barely afford even the basic commodities of life. Their clothes become worn, they have less food and less variety of food. They cannot afford to travel or take holidays, they have few luxuries and their entertainment is curtailed.

In the 1930s Britain responded to the Depression by cutting down public spending, while Germany printed more money, which led to disastrously high inflation. In Germany there were incredible stories, such as a person taking a barrowful of money to buy a loaf of bread. The value of money decreased even during the time between leaving home and arriving at the shop. Clearly inflation is a major danger in a nation where panic takes over after a financial crash. It is possible to seek stability through cost-cutting measures, and thus, at best, Britain can expect public spending to be cut. It is most likely that those on Social Security benefits will feel a major and sudden impact. The largest areas of expenditure in this area, in recent years, have been Income Support and Housing Benefit, together taking more than half of the total budget. When these allowances are cut there will be a large-scale ripple going out among those who are greatly dependent on them, which includes many young people, who have already found it difficult to get work, and many single-parent families. There are likely to be more homeless people as a result of this and more who drop out of society and live on the streets. We will see a multiplication of the problems of the homeless that we already have.

As the financial consequences take place, it is likely that sins of the past will be revealed. There will be those who look back on their broken marriages, on their wrong relationships outside marriage, on their lazy lifestyles and so on. Many of the young and unemployed will wonder if they made the best use of their education, as they now wonder if their life will ever have purpose again. As people sell off their assets it may occur to them that they made material things their gods and idols, and now their true worth is discovered.

Undoubtedly there will be resentments. Resentments against parents, against the government, against the education systems, against the church, against the Social Services, against marriage partners, even resentment against God.

There may be a shortage of food and fuel for other reasons. The world's weather patterns are less predictable than they were, and there have been many major crop failures. The oil supplies of the world are partly, at least, in the hands of those who would want to squeeze our nation and capitalise on our weakness. Islamic fundamentalism has to be a factor to consider in this, as the open declaration that Islam must dominate the world is growing in fervour, and the Muslim nations control much of the oil.

Of those who are made redundant from firms which are trying to survive, the middle management bracket will undoubtedly be hit, when those with only executive skills will find they are not needed, because computers can do their jobs. Also those with no training, offering only manual work, will find less call for their work.

There may be growing social discontent, theft, aggression, violence, looting, black-market economies, strikes, riots, gang warfare, prostitution and so on, the fruit of resentment and despair. The signs are that many young people in particular would react in this way. If a generation sees no point in life and has no values which stand as safeguards in times of difficulty, then animal instincts for personal survival, whatever the cost, and retribution against those in authority, can easily dominate.

We have seen what can happen to some extent, even in recent days, when people not only lose heart but become aggressive and violent. It is possible to visualise these things increasing as despair and resentment rise. There could be riots in the streets, followed by looting of shops and destruction of property. It is not difficult to imagine that a financial collapse could send out shock waves of poverty, panic and violence.

How will we respond?

The reaction of the British Government in the depression of the 1930s was to form a coalition and also to come out of the Gold Standard. The coalition represented a desire to share expertise in a unified scheme of building the nation. Coming out of the Gold Standard led initially to a devaluation of our currency and greater hardship. The parallel today is to remain out of a single European currency. This would leave Britain as a nation rebuilding its own foundations without seeking external props. Taken together, these two things actually give a ray of hope, even though it may seem the harder route at first. Which way we go will depend on the leadership of the nation, but we can begin to picture an opportunity for rebuilding through co-operation as we separate from the large European machinery of government.

Rebuilding does not have to be on borrowed money. We can make use of what we have. Yes, there will be simpler meals on our tables, and simpler entertainments, but there can be purpose again. There are ways of employing our young people as needs arise in the community. This will require leadership and vision, particularly from the older generations. When the financial crisis comes, we have a choice of how to respond, and we would be wise to begin our planning now. What will be exposed will be the wrong motives that have driven us over the last few decades, which can be summed up as love of money – well known to be the root of all kinds of evil – and loss of true purpose. What will be removed are the mechanisms we have created in our society which are integrated with our financial affairs. The foundations will be shaken.

The positive side of the coming collapse is the fact that we can all be brought to our senses. It may be painful, demoralising, embarrassing and shameful to see our lifestyles suffer change, but we will be in a position to discover that, in fact, bondages in our lives have been broken. We will be free to rebuild our lives on better principles even when we have suffered pain and loss.

As a preparation for the coming days, individuals and companies would be well advised to extract themselves from the spirals of speculation and debt, and to live within their means, even if this requires a simpler lifestyle and a focus on service and honest gain, rather than continuing with the selfish motives that characterise many today. At least this will minimise the shock.

Nevertheless, we are likely to go through a period in which we will all have to contribute to the rebuilding of our nation together, sharing in the needs of our families and friends. There are times of hardship ahead, but our recovery depends on how we respond.

Leadership can take the opportunity to rebuild on sound foundations. It can be like the first few years following the Second World War when the common enemy had wrought devastation, but out of which came a united response to establish the nation. Family life can be cherished once more. We could see our communities sharing what they have and working together to build things of eternal value, which don't depend on massive wealth, but more on relationships and ideals. We can take the opportunity to rediscover precious things which have been discarded as of no value, but which are of supreme value. Loyalty, honest dealing, service, training for the practical trades that bring useful and necessary facilities to society, industries that manufacture essential commodities for godly living and don't exploit people for ungodly gain or sell commodities which lure people into sinful ways, banking systems as a service rather than a control. Can the whole British nation co-operate to rebuild our society on the true foundations of the Bible and to plan for a future that God can bless?

This is God's intention for us as we seek a way out of our difficulties. If we respond correctly, he will surely help us. Above all, he is wanting us to return to being a nation which uses the Bible as an open book in our families, schools and work-places, as well as in our economy and our government. All this is possible and the opportunity to go this way is about to be given to us. It is a time for us to turn to God and his ways. As the prophecy says: 'My children, take heart, for I am with you always. Do not give up, but pray without ceasing and see the salvation of your God.' God is offering, through the pain of our trials, an opportunity for national and spiritual revival, from the ordinary household to the government and the Royal Family, and particularly to and through the church.

9
Europe

> Come out of her, my people, so that you will not share in her sins, so that you will not receive any of her plagues (Revelation 18:4).

Europe is specifically mentioned in the prophecy: 'In regard to Europe, come out of her, my dear children, for she will align herself with the Beast and thc Falsc Prophet who will arise and appear for just a short while.' This is a warning from God himself to the people of Britain who have a covenant with him like no other country in Europe has. As far as other European nations are concerned, they should also consider leaving the Union and assessing their standing before God. In this book, however, we are simply addressing the situation facing Britain in the light of the Coronation Oath.

So, while we are gathering momentum to rush into this European Alliance, God is telling us to come out. If it were not for this, we might simply argue a case for or against Europe from our own perspective. In human terms Europe has become such a complicated issue that there are many opinions, and there is much that is not clear. Of course there are advantages in seeking peace through co-operation with other countries, and seeking to trade fairly and efficiently, but the countries of Europe are moving towards stronger and stronger union, while ordinary people get lost in the cloud of uncertainty. The result will not be what many are hoping for. Nevertheless, without a clear directive we will simply drift one way or another, and the present drift towards Europe is against what is being said by God. This is a very serious situation, particularly as we have already signed agreements along the way.

More worrying, the most important point is being missed in all the paperwork passing around government circles. The negotiation for close European unity was first based on economic unity. Then it was based on political unity. Nowhere do we hear of the Coronation Oath, which makes Britain unique. Indeed, through this Oath Britain established a framework by which we could serve God, while the move towards unity with Europe puts money as a priority. God is now making this plain to us, and to make it even plainer he will show what he will do to a country which pretends to be godly but builds its foundations and alliances on finance. He will send 'a mighty earthquake' to the financial foundations in order to show their weakness and to give us a signpost back to him. This is why the European issue is important.

If we persist in breaking our covenant with God associated with the Coronation Oath, this will result in spiritual adultery with the powers of Europe. God has warned us through the prophecy that this will eventually be a covenant with the Beast and False Prophet. This is the seriousness of what we are facing.

Three major steps have been taken to form an alliance in Europe. In 1972 we signed the Accession to the Treaty of Rome. This put our key law-making and tax-gathering powers under the EEC. In 1986, the Single European Act followed, and later the Treaty for European Union was signed in 1993, in Maastricht. This has led to over 2,000 directives from the Commission in Brussels becoming law in Britain, covering every aspect of life, particularly the economy.

Along the way, the move to unity has strengthened. What was once to be an economic union is now termed the 'European Union', implying political as well as economic unity. There is now the potential to centralise the government of all member states within one European government, with each member country having a sense of national identity, but within strict limits. The laws of this central government would standardise education systems, economic systems, social systems, legal systems, industrial frameworks, our rights with our children, our political systems and eventually our religious systems.

Norman Lamont, one time Chancellor of the Exchequer, wrote in the Preface to a book called *There Is an Alternative* published by the Campaign for an Independent Britain:

> The European debate is approaching its climax in this country. What is at stake is the right of the people in democracies to govern themselves.

Burkitt, Baimbridge and Wyman, the authors of the book, state,

> The Maastricht Treaty committed the EU to evolve towards eventual political, economic and monetary

> union, which would turn Parliament at Westminster into a mere assembly rubber stamping 'union' legislation and acting as a peripheral local authority, dealing with a remote centralised bureaucracy operating hundreds of miles away.

They argue coherently that there *are* viable economic alternatives to continuing with this union. They also demonstrate that there has already been enormous expenditure in the ups and downs of attempts at moving towards monetary union. For Great Britain, between 1985 and 1994 there has been the equivalent of £145 billion trade deficit with other EU members, a net contribution of £30 billion to the EU budget, a loss of at least £68 billion as a result of ERM membership between 1990 and 1992 (we later pulled out of the ERM), and an additional spending of 8% of Britain's annual income (GDP) to carry out its obligations to directives from the Commission in Brussels.

The issue of the sovereignty of member nations is a topic which is hotly discussed. Sovereignty is the ability of a member state to make its own laws. Clearly sovereignty is going to be gradually weakened as centralised government establishes itself. Article 2 of the Treaty of Rome, amended by Article G(B) of the Maastricht Treaty reads:

> The Community shall have as its task, by establishing a common market and an economic and monetary union and by implementing the common policies or activities referred to in Article 3 and 3a, to promote throughout the Community a harmonious and balanced development of economic activities, sustainable and non-inflationary growth respecting the environment, a high degree of convergence of economic performance, a high level of employment and of social protection, the

> raising of the standard of living and quality of life, and economic and social cohesion and solidarity among Member States.

Such aims seem pure at first glance, but we must ask what it might take to attempt to implement them and whether it is within the ability of men and women to do so, particularly with unwieldy central bureaucracy. Will we not in fact feel the effects in the old-fashioned corner shops of our nation, closed down because they are not cost-effective? Will we discover reductions in personalised local services and trades, which become too small-scale to contribute to the larger machine of industry? Will we see our children's education streamlined to emphasise the priorities of the new Europe, where indoctrination of new ideals will take over? Every grain of wheat grown in Britain will come under the management of the European Commission and lose its value somewhere along the line, as too will the simple things of community life, which will be seen to be non-cost-effective. As it says in Article A of the Treaty:

> This Treaty marks a new stage in the process of creating an ever closer union among the peoples of Europe, in which decisions are taken as closely as possible to the citizen.

It is anticipated that these decisions will be of benefit but, as many predict, the union will be a hard and harsh regime so that, in times of difficulty, the ordinary citizen will be tightly squeezed.

The 'Social Chapter', relating mainly to the workplace and trade union rights, has been resisted by the Tory Government in Britain, but could be approved by a Labour Government. Once approved it could not be reversed by another government. So, as days proceed and opinions vary at government level, there is a machinery moving forward which will gradually draw the nations of Europe into a tighter and tighter union. The Prime Minister, representing the Crown, may enter into binding commitments with the European governmental structure. These agreements will have legal force without prior approval of Parliament or even the Cabinet. Community laws passed by the Council of Ministers or European Commission take precedence over laws passed at Westminster, and are enforceable by British courts of law. We have already gone a long way down the road.

The balance of power

The democracy of England goes back to the Magna Carta of 1215 when some powers were taken from the monarch of England by the barons. The Divine Right of Kings ended with the Civil War. Eventually the balance between monarchy, church and Parliament came about as our national model, and the Coronation Oath stands as the declaration that Britain will be a Protestant nation, reflecting the values of God. This has major implications for the way we should maintain our country's laws to honour God, our education systems to bring up our children according to the teaching of the Bible, our political system which should set its agendas in prayer before God and so on, with the Bible as the open book of the nation.

Queen Elizabeth I stated, 'To no power whatsoever is my crown subject save to that of Christ the King of kings.' Queen Elizabeth II, following all monarchs since 1688, promised to 'maintain the laws of God and the true profession of the gospel'. Though these traditions seem antiquated and will be a barrier to full integration into Europe, they have been our safeguard. Behind the scenes there are many discussions going on as to how to modify the Coronation Oath, or remove the monarchy and the House of Lords and to disestablish the Church of England. All this would be an unravelling of our commitments to God so that we can make commitments to economic, political and eventually religious unity with Europe. Blind Britain may not see the significance of this or give it any attention, but it is important to God.

Once in the European community, we will gradually be unable to run our country on anything but the principles of the European Union. In effect we would compromise all that we have achieved socially, educationally, legally and morally over the years that we have had a Protestant tradition as our benchmark. Though we have already slipped away from the standards that God would have in our society, a move into Europe would eventually break our covenant with him completely.

Ultimately, the decision to enter Europe should not depend on economics but on whether this is what God wants us to do. We gave him the right to speak and guide us by setting up our principles of government in the way that we have. Unfortunately, many of today's prominent leaders neither expect him to speak nor seek him in prayer for the most part. When he does speak they will have difficulties believing it and difficulties obeying it. The country should be called to prayer so that we can confirm the way God wants us to go.

In an earlier chapter we outlined what the European monster could become. It is interesting how similar the words of the prophecy are to the passage in the book of Revelation quoted at the beginning of this chapter. The book of Revelation points to a time when a world government will emerge which is controlled by satanic powers. A unity will be brought about which will dominate the economies of the world, the political structures of the world, and where there will also be a world religion integrated with them. This is everything that Britain set out to avoid when we made our Coronation Oath. This union will be so dominant that no one will be able to buy or sell if a special mark is not taken on the forehead or right hand. There are signs that present-day technology could enable such biblical prophecy to be fulfilled.

We are rapidly moving into a cashless society that will change dramatically all of our ways of buying and selling. It could impose strict controls on us, by means of computer marks on our body or small computer chip implants. A computer mark can be read directly in shops, banks, theatres, hospitals, or anywhere where official records are kept, including records of criminal offences.

Computer marks like this could replace plastic credit cards and other identity cards which can be damaged, forged or lost, so it would seem that they would be a convenience and a safeguard. But it all sounds very similar to the description in Revelation, which tells us that anyone taking the 'mark' will form an alliance with Satan and his world system – an alliance that would prevent that person from receiving salvation through the shed blood of Jesus Christ. Could such a system be coming to Europe?

One world religion

While political and economic unity are at the forefront of present day considerations regarding unity with Europe, we would suggest that moves towards uniformity in religion could also follow. The Christian foundation of Britain, demonstrated by the Coronation Oath, was built on the Protestant Reformation of the sixteenth century, and men like Ridley and Latimer gave their lives to establish Protestant Christianity in Britain. Fox's *Book of Martyrs* tells us that just as the light was put to the faggots to burn these two men at the stake, Bishop Latimer was heard to remark to Dr Ridley:

> Be of good cheer, Master Ridley; and play the man. We shall this day, by God's grace, light up such a candle in England, as I trust will never be put out.

Surely we should be wary of aligning ourselves with a Europe that might come once again under the domination of Roman Catholic teaching and practice.

There is also a subtle form of false spirituality developing in the world today. It is called the New Age Movement, and is a blend of many world religions, reminding us of ancient Babylon. It is becoming acceptable in many countries and among many people because it demands no radical change in a person. It teaches that we are already part of God. Such an idea has no place in the Christian faith, which declares mankind's desperate need for a saviour. Such a spurious spirituality, with strong humanistic ideals and promises of unity, could become very acceptable throughout the West. Are we about to see a one-world religion? Are we on the brink of breaking our covenant with God in order to make an alliance with a power base which is serving the devil, no less?

In Joshua chapter 9, we read how Joshua made a treaty for peace with some people called Gibeonites. The treaty came about by deception, and even though it was against God's will for Israel, because they had made it they had to keep it. We have made the beginnings of a treaty with Europe which is a mistake. We are in a similar position to the covenant people of Israel at the time of Joshua; so what shall we do, for we must keep our agreements? We should seek God earnestly in prayer over Europe, and then we might see the salvation of our God.

Which way forward?

The best thing that could happen is that we be asked to resign from Europe, or that an offer of resignation be accepted. Perhaps our economic Woe will bring this about.

In the short term it would be right to give the people of Britain a referendum and to lay these issues before them. Then we could be responsible for taking our serious decisions together. If we find a way out of Europe then it will provide an opportunity to renew our covenant with God. In view of the treaties we have already made, it is going to be difficult to come out without the Lord God acting on our behalf. One possible way would be for him to prompt the Europeans to decide that they no longer want us to be a part of the new European Union that they are building together. Alternatively, they could nullify previous treaties by bringing in a new treaty – which we would have the opportunity *not* to sign – incorporating the previous three treaties, together with a new federal intent to create a United States of Europe. If we do come out of Europe then it will be an opportunity to reconsider our commitment to the British Commonwealth. When we made steps towards Europe, surely we neglected our responsibilities to our Commonwealth partners.

The Former Speaker of the House of Commons, Lord Tonypandy, wrote of the deception that has taken us this far. In *The Times* newspaper of 24th April 1995 he wrote:

> The current slide towards a single currency threatens both our economical and political independence, and thus our sovereignty. Subterfuge and half-truths have been used to persuade the nation that neither our sovereignty nor our relationship with the Commonwealth is endangered. . . . For more than 600 years Speakers of the House of Commons have fiercely defended the supremacy of the Westminster Parliament. As one whose privilege it was to follow humbly in the steps of the past, I call upon our nation to awake, and to demand that the voice of our people shall be heard before the next intergovernmental conference takes irrevocable decisions affecting our sovereignty. A referendum conducted before, and not after, further decisions are taken is our elementary right. This is the only sure way to prevent our parliamentary sovereignty, our judicial system, and our Commonwealth relationships from being grievously undermined.

In weighing up all these things we might picture two possible futures. The one is the building out of hardship which results from God's judgement on our nation. The other is the false hope of a stable future, maintaining as much as we can of the status quo in

Britain, by continuing our thrust into Europe. The first is a path of recovery with God, which requires faith. The second is trusting in the ways of man, independent of God, which will lead to following false gods. As Joshua once said, when there was such a choice before the Children of Israel as they crossed over the Jordan into the Promised Land, with seemingly impossible tasks ahead:

> If serving the Lord seems undesirable to you, then choose for yourselves this day whom you will serve, whether the gods your forefathers served beyond the River, or the gods of the Amorites, in whose land you are living. But as for me and my household, we will serve the Lord (Joshua 24:15).

10

'Great' Britain

> Blessed is the nation whose God is the Lord (Psalm 33:12).

God has been gracious to Britain in the past. If there have been times of blessing and protection then it is on account of God's goodness. God helped many of our nation to seek righteousness and justice, combating the evil that has also been evident in every generation. Our nation has tasted the fruits of righteousness. Our history books are full of men and women whose goal was to make Great Britain *great*. The world has witnessed how we have cared for the poor, fed the hungry, educated our children, governed with justice and compassion, kept evil at a distance, organised our work force, cared for the sick, and honoured the God of the Bible. Those who can look back to a blessed heritage might be stirred to remember these things – especially those of older generations.

We established laws which protected us from pornography and violence, that set the marriage contract as a sacred covenant between men and women, that brought justice and deterrent to men of violence and lawlessness, that encouraged fair dealing in the market-place and kept the Sabbath day holy.

We have never been a totally righteous nation, of course, but the strand of righteousness that has been evident in Britain has led to our being blessed by God, and by considering the positive aspects of our history we can learn lessons for the future.

Many from the older generations in Britain remember family life at its best. People had time to talk, to make plans, to value each other and their time together. They made their own entertainment and enjoyed times of pleasure within the local community. There was time to walk out and enjoy the natural world. There was time for hobbies and constructive interests.

At school, our children were taught about the Creator of the universe. They were taught about the world of nature in a way that honoured God. Science was a servant and not a master. School assemblies were the focal point of the day, when everyone was taught about God the Father and the Lord Jesus Christ. While it might be argued that this was sometimes just a case of going through the motions of religion, we would argue that those days saw the blessing and protection of God on our schools. Sadly that is not the case today. The Ten Commandments were taught and the Lord's Prayer was said daily. Children were taught the history of Britain so that they would know the rich heritage into which they were born. They were taught the path of service instead of personal gain. There was security for our children in those days. They knew the bounds of right and wrong and had absolute standards in everything.

Ordinary people were not as wealthy as they are now, but they looked forward to the special celebrations of the year. Summer holidays, Christmas, birthdays – there was something special about our celebrations. Sundays in Britain were quiet family times. A hush and stillness came over the nation, in a way that was full of peace. There was a refreshment to our inner beings as we rested for that one day. On a Sunday the church bells rang out calling the people to come to worship God. This was a feature of our national life. There were amazing peaks in our history of worshipping God, such as in Wales, shortly before the First World War, and just after the Welsh Revival. There, in the mining villages of Wales, the only people not going to church were the sick. One would look out of the window as one prepared to go to Sunday morning service, and a sea of people would be filling the roadways, making their way to chapel.

Britain was second to none in her industries and trades. The standards of safety among our work-force, and our quality of service and manufactured products led the world. Our craftsmen were trained to the highest levels. Care and skill were applied in every area. Stonemasons, wood-workers, bricklayers, plumbers, electricians, tool-makers, metal-workers, farmers, bakers, carpet fitters, coach-builders, upholsterers, book-binders – all were skilled men whose vision was to establish a quality of life which was safe, secure and healthy, with high quality products and service. Nurses, doctors, health-care workers, teachers, ministers of the church, solicitors and others, were respected professional people who established a framework of health in body, soul, mind and spirit, and gave us a vision and a hope.

Now we don't want to look back on the past and over-glamorise it, and there has never been perfection. Yet we know that today absolute standards have slipped, laws that protected have been reversed, discord, disorder, selfishness, materialism and lawlessness are growing. Britain once had a blessed heritage. Why was this? The answer is simple. Through our law structures, which brought in principles of righteousness which filtered down through society, we were building on the firm foundations of the Bible. It was these foundations that mattered and God helped us to build while they were in place. This is the principle of Scripture. There is no nation that can build itself up in righteousness, peace and justice without God. Yet when our foundations are right he has shown us that he will help us. 'Blessed is the nation whose God is the Lord' is a proven principle in Britain. When we built on the foundations of the Ten Commandments we were blessed in our families, in our work-place, in our schools, in our hospitals, in our industry and in our government.

Once it was possible to call our country *Great* Britain without a sense of shame. The greatness of Britain was always associated with her desire to serve the one true God and to have the principles of the Bible taught and applied in every important area of national life. The Ten Commandments were learned by every schoolchild and were in the minds of lawmakers as they established Britain's framework of government.

This was so engrained in our national life that it was like an unwritten constitution. Christianity came to Britain in the early centuries after Jesus Christ and, from then on, we have been influenced by the teaching of the Bible and became known as the people of the Book.

Thinking rationally about this, if a nation sets out to serve God then it is only natural that the principles of the Bible will be of the utmost importance. Where else would such a nation get its principles? Thus while the Bible has been highly prized in Britain we have also had leaders who referred to it in all major decisions.

One of the present authors remembers receiving a Bible on entry to secondary school in the 1950s, as was commonplace in those days. It was a gift from the Monmouthshire Education Committee, and the only book that was presented to us as a gift. The inscription in the front cover read, 'This Bible is given to you to mark the beginning of your secondary education in Monmouthshire. We trust that the faith which it embodies will always help, comfort and guide you.' It was said at the time that our education was the best in the world. Success was surely linked to the Christian emphasis that our leaders brought to the nation.

The Revd David Gardner commented in his paper, 'Whither Britannia?':

> When [I] was a boy, the Law of the Land was absolutely in line with, and identical with, The Law of God as stated in the Ten Commandments, and the Ten Commandments were absolutely in line with the Law of the Land so that it was impossible to tell the difference the one from the other.

This is a remarkable statement which few, if any, other countries can claim. He also made a brief and useful analysis of the way the Bible became the backbone of our legal system as it developed over many centuries.

This is included in the second book of the trilogy, *The Trumpet Sounds for Britain*. It is from this trilogy that we have drawn material for use in this chapter.

The making of laws

The moral origins of English common law came from the early Christian roots over fifteen hundred years ago. The foundation of our law was the existence of God and the lordship of Jesus Christ. The three most powerful influences which moulded Western civilisation as a whole were Roman civil law, Roman canon law and English common law. Eventually, English law continued to develop and to become the most Christian of them all. In the earlier years of Christianity these law structures grew alongside the Christian faith and were the means whereby heathen laws of barbaric people were abolished and savage customs were remodelled along more humane lines.

The Roman Emperor Justinian (AD 527–565) drew up the code of law called 'Corpus Juris Civilis' based on Christian principles. This law code was to have immediate and continuous influence throughout the then Roman Empire. The rigour and harshness of the old laws had been tempered through the influence of the Christian faith in the drawing up of the new code. The direct influence on English law began when Augustine landed at Kent in AD 597 and King Ethelbert converted to Christianity. By the time of Alfred, English law was being modelled along Christian lines, which he then codified into a coherent system. The Ten Commandments were written into these laws.

The development of English law along Christian lines continued through Henry II, the Plantagenet (1154–1189), who made a choice for the English law system when he arrived from the continent. This was seen as a major landmark. Winston Churchill wrote of Henry II, 'No man has left a deeper mark upon our laws and institutions than he ... His fame will live with the English Constitution, and the English Common law.' This system of law, said Churchill, 'in the mass, still governs the English-speaking peoples today. Its main outlines were not to be altered.' These were the origins of Christian Britain of which other eminent lawyers have brought confirmation. This was, for example, clearly expressed by an address given by George Polson QC, Recorder of Essex, when he said, 'The true basis of English common law is Christianity, which itself was founded on older principles which are enshrined in Judaism.' The reference to Judaism is the link to the teaching of the Old Testament of the Bible, which has the Ten Commandments at its heart.

This is the background from which the Coronation Oath emerged, where the incoming monarch swears the solemn oath before Almighty God, promising to the utmost of his or her power, to 'maintain the Laws of God, the true profession of the Gospel and the Protestant reformed religion established by law'.

So there is ample evidence from our historians that Britain set out to establish herself as a Christian country through her legal systems, and this has been the over-riding principle in all of her dealings in the world for centuries. The Ten Commandments are the basic starting point for the laws of God written into the Bible. They are clearly stated and straightforward to understand and apply within our legal system and our way of life.

The fruits of righteousness

Perhaps the most dramatic years of Christian impact in Britain were also the years of prominence of the British Empire. It was said that the sun never went down on the British Empire. We established a Christian base in Britain that had the potential to teach the world about the one true God and his Son, the Lord Jesus Christ. Our impact was dramatic though imperfect, of course. Our imperfections have left their own residual effect, but it is not the point of this chapter to highlight this. Our point is to bring a reminder of a Christian heritage that we once had and the blessings that came from this.

Imperfect Christianity and its witness was still blessed. This gives us hope for the future, and a pointer to the direction we should go. We should seek to deepen our Christian convictions rather than lessen them now that we are at a time of luke-warmness and apostasy, which God is not blessing.

It was Christian influence which humanised the British prison system. Men were seen as created in God's image and not to be treated like animals, even while serving just sentences in prison for crime. Christianity brought the balance between justice and responsibility to the individual, removing the cruelty from previous penal systems. John Howard, William Wilberforce and Elizabeth Fry are among the household names of people whose commitment to reform brought righteousness to our prisons.

Education for all was another area which grew out

of our Christian heritage. The Sunday school movement of the late 1700s concentrated on reading and writing, with the Bible at the centre. A great revival of Christianity had occurred in the 1700s which sparked a national desire among all people to read the Bible. This desire to read the Bible overflowed into a desire for education in general. Voluntary schooling sprang up everywhere, and in 1870 the Board Schools Act was designed to draw together and extend what the voluntary schools were doing. This had been preceded by Lord Shaftesbury's Factory Act in 1847, freeing the nation from child labour, with one of the motives being 'that children should be freed, and educated nobly to take their place as intelligent, useful, healthy and happy citizens in a Christian State'.

Similarly it was the great Christian awakening of the eighteenth century that inspired the growth of hospital care in Britain. Out of this revival of Christianity came men and women whose lives were changed through the gospel message. This gave them a zeal for spiritual rather than materialistic ideals. The voluntary hospital system of Britain emerged supported by free-will gifts. This was unique in the systems of the world and led to major achievements and improvements in public health, which have formed the basis for the modern developments of health care in our nation.

The purpose in life that true Christian faith gave to the people of Britain brought vision for a range of voluntary social service organisations, welfare systems and other national facilities. In these we see the origins of modern social welfare which has been of great benefit to all men and women in Britain. The pioneers of the nineteenth century not only led

Britain, but set an example for the whole world to follow.

The abolition of the slave trade was another major contribution by Christians who understood the value of all men because of what the Bible teaches. The horrible sufferings of Negro slaves, who had been treated more like animals than people, were brought to focus for twenty hard years, pioneered by Wilberforce and Thurlow in Paliament, supported by Granville Sharp, Clarkson and Zachary Macaulay outside, assisted by Pitt and Fox. The Act of 1807 finally began a process which resulted in the slave trade being abolished in British dominions.

When the industrial revolution arrived, Christian influence was brought to the factories by men who understood the value of a human being and the righteousness of God. Lord Shaftesbury inspired the movement towards the Factory Act of 1833, regulating the hours that could be worked by women and young people, and protected young children from being employed. This was one among many Acts in factories, mines and industry in general, which form the basis of modern industrial management and care. The men behind these Acts had the Christian faith as their benchmark. It is important to recognise how the tendency of human society without God is always towards selfishness, exploitation and greed – quite the opposite to the commandments of God. Because the benchmarks of Christianity were embedded in the characters of men and women, and in our law structure, it was possible to bring restraints against these natural tendencies of mankind. Britain had a structure which breathed godliness within all her institutions. Queen Victoria was able to put in a message to two

African chiefs: 'England has become great and happy by the knowledge of the true God and Jesus Christ.'

The historian J.R. Green wrote in his well-known book *A Short History of the English People* published in 1899, concerning the link between the revival of Christianity in the eighteenth century and the character of Britain's society in the nineteenth century:

> . . . a religious revival burst forth . . . which changed in a few years the whole temper of English society. The Church was restored to life and activity. Religion carried to the hearts of the people a fresh spirit of moral zeal, while it purified our literature and our manners. A new philanthropy reformed our prisons, infused clemency and wisdom into our penal laws, abolished the slave-trade, and gave the first impulse to popular education (pp. 736–737).

The curriculums of our schools did try to honour the God of creation. As recently as the 1944 Education Act, all schools, by law, were expected to have a daily act of worship to the God who has protected and inspired us over these many centuries.

Human nature

The Ten Commandments provide the basis of God's law structure. They are perfect in themselves, but the Bible teaches that the laws of God are like a guide and protection to bring us to Jesus Christ, the end point and fulfilment of it all.

By having godly laws on our statute books, we are in a position for God to bless us and lead us and our children to salvation for the next life. The nature of human beings is to go against the laws of God, and without some restraining influence we will become corrupt and barbaric. Of themselves, these laws do not change human nature. A nation with godly laws, however, will provide a framework which can lead to blessing from God and protection, while the process of spiritual conversion can come about through the sovereign work of the Holy Spirit in the lives of individuals. Righteous laws bring true freedom to a nation by defining the boundaries of behaviour. All true freedom has boundaries which, once known, give freedom of movement within their framework. There is glorious freedom when we know our bounds. This is so for a child who can play safely and freely when the boundaries of what is allowed and where it can go are known. This is also true for adults in all areas of life.

During the 1700s there was a great spiritual revival led by the Wesleys and George Whitefield, in which this nation heard and responded to the gospel message of Jesus Christ. It was out of this spiritual revival that men and women of the 1800s emerged to transform the character of the nation into one that was to be God-centred in our homes, schools, factories, hospitals and government, a heritage which has held firm until the present day. Now, however, we are rejecting the Ten Commandments one by one. Casting off the laws of God, however, eventually leads to growing rebellion against God and disorder of every kind in a nation. 'Where there is no revelation, the people cast off restraint' (Proverbs 29:18).

Natural man does not want to rest on the Sabbath, worship God the Creator, or even believe in him. Natural man covets and steals and blasphemes, commits adultery and even murders, when restraint is taken away. This is why the righteousness of Britain cannot be maintained by its laws imposed externally only. An internal transformation of human beings is also required.

Jesus Christ taught us that all God's teachings hang on two principles: loving God with all our hearts and our neighbours as ourselves. Love is first to God and then to mankind. Love of this sort cannot be manufactured by law books. It is a gift of God when he brings new birth through salvation. Then we see that the Ten Commandments are like a spectrum of this love. They start with the highest honour of God and end with the most sensitive respect for our neighbour, whereby we don't even desire the smallest thing that belongs to our neighbour. In the scope of these principles lie the family relationships at the centre of a believing community – right relationships between husband and wife and between children and parents. The fourth commandment is the link between heaven and earth, whereby we take a day of rest once a week, trusting God, worshipping him and blending our response to him with our family life and relationships. These principles are deeper than any law code of a country and not limited to any particular human era. They reflect the willing heart condition of men and women who are truly converted to belief in Christ. Without such conversion the laws will only be restraints on our carnal natures. This restraint is extremely important and the reason for the great progress Britain made in the world, but the higher call, to willing obedience and love for God and one another, is our true goal.

In summary, we can see from the history of Britain that God's laws have been our safeguard for nearly two thousand years. God has blessed us not only with prosperity and honour but with spiritual revivals which have changed the character of our people through many generations, causing them to desire to follow God's ways. The Great Awakening of Christianity in Britain in the eighteenth century brought the means by which Britain achieved her status of greatness in the nineteenth century. This, in turn, formed the basis on which leaders of the twentieth century could build. It has not been a perfect path, and our transgressions have brought hardship, but it is an identifiable path of growth and blessing, making us like no other nation. Whenever we have slipped, God has helped us back. So far.

The righteousness of Britain through its law system has been blessed by God. Now we are changing our laws. Relative morality and false spirituality are coming in like a flood. Boundaries are being removed, and false gods are rising, leading to lawlessness. We are moving out of God's blessings, which keep and honour a nation, and as a result, many people are also in danger of missing out on the fulness of salvation, and preparation for the next life. What a thorough catastrophe it will be if we undo all that God did through men and women in previous generations, who honoured his laws and built up a righteousness in Britain that could be blessed.

It is not too late to recover the blessings that we experienced in previous generations, the blessings of family life, of the work-place, of our industries, on our farms, in our schools, in our entertainment, through the radio, newspapers, television, films and theatres. It is not too late to recover, but we must seek God with all our heart as men and women have done in previous generations, loving what is right and hating what is wrong. Just as men and women in the past gave their lives in service, to establish our righteous laws, so it is possible for that flame and zeal to fill the hearts of individuals today. From the family through to government, God is looking out for men and women whom he can use to re-establish what has been lost. How do we begin? By prayer and by opening and reading the Bible. This is something we can all do.

We will leave the last word of this chapter to William Wilberforce, who wrote in *A Practical View of Christianity* in 1797:

> I must confess equally boldly that my own solid hopes for the well-being of my country depend, not so much on her navies and armies, nor on the wisdom of her rulers, nor on the spirit of her people, as on the persuasion that she still contains many who love and obey the Gospel of Christ. I believe that their prayers may yet prevail.

11

Unrighteous Britain

> They were broken off because of unbelief, and you stand by faith. Do not be arrogant, but be afraid. For if God did not spare the natural branches, he will not spare you either. Consider therefore the kindness and sternness of God: sternness to those who fell, but kindness to you, provided that you continue in his kindness. Otherwise, you also will be cut off (Romans 11:20–22).

> For it is time for judgement to begin with the family of God (1 Peter 4:17).

The prophecy about the coming Woe concerns both the nation and the church. Because of the growth of unrighteousness in the nation, the Lord God is going to bring judgement which will be both a physical sign in the form of an earthquake, and a financial collapse. When this occurs it must be seen as an opportunity for the nation to turn to God. First, however, the church itself must turn back to him so that it can be the means by which God speaks to the nation in order to bring her to repentance.

The nation is on the brink of turning away from God into an ungodly alliance with Europe, breaking its Coronation Oath covenant. Already many of the righteous laws have been reversed and God's laws are broken daily by millions of people. Sadly, the heart of this nation is no longer Christian.

Since the abandoning of censorship, almost every programme on the television must be monitored for scenes of sex or violence. There is unlimited exploitation of the young through media channels, so that a tide of permissiveness, including drug abuse, sex and violence is cultivated. Every child in the country may be influenced by the tide of evil that comes through films, television and other media. This is reflected in the growth of sexual adventures outside of marriage and a growing tide of violence.

In our schools the text books which consider social issues do not have a strong teaching of right and wrong. Controversial issues are raised as matters for discussion, whereby children are encouraged to form their own opinions. This is a symptom of the relative morality which has come into our nation. As a consequence we see increasing numbers of teenage pregnancies and teenage girls seeking abortions. Moral absolutes have been eroded and youngsters are no longer encouraged to flee from fornication.

The gay and lesbian lifestyle is presented as if it were an acceptable alternative lifestyle. This has grown from the 1950s through the Gay Rights Movement. At first the emphasis was on fairness to a minority group, but now the whole movement has gathered momentum and publicly proclaims that 'gay is good'. Large numbers of people are mobilised to promote their ideas, and pressure is put on public figures to 'come out' and identify themselves as homosexual or lesbian. Now we have the Lesbian and Gay

Christian Movement which found approval for marking its twentieth anniversary with a service of celebration in Southwark Cathedral. Practising homosexuals have been ordained, and unions between homosexual partners have been acknowledged and approved. All this in spite of the clear teaching of Scripture that such things are an abomination in God's eyes (Leviticus 18:22).

One fifth of all family units consists of a single parent. It is estimated that by the year 2000 there will be 1.7 million single parents in Britain. There is growing domestic violence in many families. There is growing adultery. Many choose not to marry. Around 25% of all single women were cohabiting in the mid-1990s, despite the statistics which show that relationships of this kind last, on average, less than three years. The divorce rate in Britain has been rising steadily over the last decade to levels that would have been unimaginable to previous generations. The average age for divorce now centres on the mid-thirties. These are the men and women who began life in the 1960s, inheriting the teaching of relative morality and the permissiveness which characterised those years.

The accumulated effect of marriage break-up, single-parent families and other factors, such as unemployment, puts a tremendous strain on the economy of the country. God is not blessing us, and we should be considering what we have done and how we can put things right.

In this chapter we will consider how the Ten Commandments are disregarded by most of the nation and we will consider some of the laws that have taken the godly restraint away from the nation. Those who read these things who are not members of the church should begin to consider how they might respond in their own lives. The main point of the message, however, is to those who are in the church. It is time for the church to repent of her slumber and to wake up to her responsibility as prophet and watchman to the nation. It is time for her to consider how far the sins of the world have come into the church and compromised her power to proclaim the gospel message. She is not a sufficiently pure vessel to be to the nation the salt and light that are so desperately needed. It is time for her to remember our Christian heritage, recognise the urgency of the hour and intercede for this nation once more.

The decline into unrighteousness of the nation as a whole has affected the church. There must be a time of repentance from all the worldliness and sin that is in the church before we will be ready to lead the nation into repentance. This includes unrighteousness in our financial and business practices, our family life, following after false spiritual experiences and general neglect of the application of Bible truths to our lives. It is time for each Christian and each congregation to seek God for the particular areas of repentance to which they are being called, so that our Christian witness becomes strong in this day of crisis for our nation.

Warning signs to the church

In July 1984 there was a lightning strike on York Minster. The weather records showed that Britain was covered by clear blue skies on the day of David Jenkins' consecration as Bishop of Durham.

David Jenkins was already well known for his liberal views and open denial of foundational Bible truths. In the clear blue sky of that day just one small cloud was seen which travelled across to Durham and out of which came a lightning bolt of such power that the newly installed lightning conductor of York Minster was useless and immense damage occurred to the Minster only hours after the service of consecration. Surely God was showing his displeasure to the leadership of the Church of England concerning the liberality and unbelief represented by this choice of bishop.

Another sign was the fire in Windsor Castle in 1992. The fire began in the private chapel where the Queen herself was confirmed, and went on to destroy many of the material treasures in the castle. This has been interpreted as a sign from God relating to the compromise with other faiths that is taking place in the Church of England and by the Queen, who is the leader of the State Church. A multi-faith emphasis has come to the annual Commonwealth Day service in Westminster Abbey, in the very place where the Queen took the Coronation Oath. She promised to maintain Protestant Christianity in Britain, but has opened the way for multi-faith worship, despite warnings from her subjects, including a petition signed by 77,000 Christians. During the 1990s each Commonwealth Day service has contained contributions from many faiths including Sikhs, Muslims, Hindus and Buddhists as well as Christians. Each has read from their own scriptures in a way that implies that there is a common faith underlying them, and that they all serve the same god. This is quite contrary to the truth and compromises the Christian faith in a way that is surely an abomination to the one true God.

The breaking of the Ten Commandments

The extent of Britain's unrighteousness in the present generation can be seen by how far we have drifted from the Ten Commandments. Let us look at the commandments as recorded in Exodus 20 and see how we have broken them all.

The first commandment

> I am the Lord your God, who brought you out of Egypt, out of the land of slavery. You shall have no other gods before me.

Britain now has an open door to other gods, and these gods are approved by our leaders. The law has even legalised witchcraft. The Prince of Wales is claiming that he wants to defend faith, rather than the Protestant Christian faith alone. These are just a few examples of how we are serving other gods.

The second commandment

> You shall not make for yourself an idol in the form of anything in heaven above or on the earth beneath or in the waters below. You shall not bow down to them or worship them; for I the Lord your God am a jealous God, punishing the children for the sin of the fathers to the third and fourth generation of those who hate me, but showing love to a thousand generations of those who love me and keep my commandments.

The idols of other religions that Britain once kept at a distance are now set up in our land. Furthermore the subtle idols of a materialistic society have become the goals and gods of this age. We have allowed sport, money, property, cars, computers, televisions, art, science and entertainment to become more important in our lives than Jesus Christ and our relationship with him.

The third commandment

> You shall not misuse the name of the Lord your God, for the Lord will not hold anyone guiltless who misuses his name.

The Lord's name is misused daily. For too long 'Jesus Christ' has been a swear word. Marriage vows, oaths in courts of law, and the Coronation Oath are all examples of oaths taken in the name of God. If they are broken, the Lord's name is taken in vain.

The fourth commandment

> Remember the Sabbath day by keeping it holy. Six days you shall labour and do all your work, but the seventh day is a Sabbath to the Lord your God. On it you shall not do any work, neither you, nor your son or daughter, nor your manservant or maidservant, nor your animals, nor the alien within your gates. For in six days the Lord made the heavens and the earth, the sea, and all that is in them, but he rested on the seventh day. Therefore the Lord blessed the Sabbath day and made it holy.

The Sabbath day is no longer kept. This demonstrates to God that we do not believe in him or want to worship him. We do not believe that he created the world in six days, and we do not want to celebrate the fact that on the seventh day he rested, blessing this day and making it holy. We do not look forward to the time of Jesus' return to reign, which will give the fullest meaning to the Sabbath rest, when he will bring in his kingdom of peace to all who believe in him. The recent Sunday Trading Bill demonstrates the lukewarmness of this nation towards God and the fourth commandment. We do not value the other side of this commandment either, which acknowledges the rightness of six days of work.

The fifth commandment

> Honour your father and mother, so that you may live long in the land the Lord your God is giving you.

Parents are despised and not honoured. Discipline has broken down in the home, and youngsters no longer respect the aged and mature members of society. We hear of children terrorising neighbourhoods and schools.

The sixth commandment

> You shall not murder.

Abortion was legalised in 1967, and by 1969 there were 50,000 abortions in a single year. A total of three million lives had been taken by 1989, and by 1992 the yearly death rate had risen to nearly 200,000. The number of abortions per year continues to be between 170,000 and 200,000. This means that, on current trends, over five million babies will have been aborted as the century draws to a close.

The seventh commandment

> You shall not commit adultery.

Marriage has been cheapened and it is now unusual for marriage vows to be kept for a lifetime. Divorce, which God hates, is common. There are also many couples living together with no intention of marrying.

The eighth commandment

> You shall not steal.

This nation exploits the poorer nations of the world by not paying enough for their produce. Employees steal from their employers – time, stationery, personal telephone calls. They fiddle their expense sheets and wrongly claim sickness pay. Social security benefit frauds abound, as do insurance frauds. Petty crimes like fare dodging, shoplifting and failure to pay bills are on the increase.

The ninth commandment

> You shall not give false testimony against your neighbour.

We have become a selfish nation and no longer care for our neighbours. In the media truth is secondary to sensation, and a person's character can be destroyed by harmful public accusation. 'Trial by press' is common.

The tenth commandment

> You shall not covet your neighbour's house. You shall not covet your neighbour's wife, or his manservant or maidservant, his ox or donkey, or anything that belongs to your neighbour.

We have gone beyond coveting. People are seeking their own ends and desiring *more* than their neighbours. The National Lottery encourages this desire.

We have gone this far from the Ten Commandments, and we have gone away from God himself and the greatest of all commandments, to love him with all our heart, soul, mind and strength, and our neighbours as ourselves. The plumb-line has been set against the people of Britain today, and we are not upright in God's sight. To love God is to obey his commandments, just as his love for us is to actively bless us and prosper us, if we put ourselves in a position for him to do so. We will realise how active his love has been towards us when he withdraws his favour from us. Then it will be too late. We will know what it is to be isolated, lacking protection, with no sense of well-being. We will feel deserted, for the most holy God cannot protect what is evil; he will let evil run its own course in our lives if that is our choice – having warned us, as a father does the rebellious child whom he loves.

Unrighteous laws

To emphasise these points even further, we can consider the way in which the laws of Britain have been changed in this generation to open the way to breaking the commandments. Here is a list of some of the laws that stand as witness to our having reversed our righteous standing before God as a nation.

1957

The abolition of the law prohibiting witchcraft was passed. This has resulted in a rising interest in the occult, including among schoolchildren. It is now legal to commit the most horrendous blasphemies against God. The rise of Satanism, in all its forms, has followed on from this.

1959

The Obscene Publications Act was passed, followed by an Amendment in 1964. This Act altered a number of key issues from the original Act of 1857. It allows much more licence in publishing what had previously been classed as obscene material, if the contents are considered to be in the interests of science, literature, arts or learning. In effect this has opened the way for removal of censorship in many areas that had been protected in previous generations.

1963

Betting, Gaming and Lotteries Act was passed. Betting at licensed offices was made legal. This, and other acts which followed, opened the way for the wide range of gambling which is now a part of our national life, including bingo halls and gaming machines, as well as betting on horse races and in many other ways. Covetousness is encouraged by gambling, which can lead to hardship in families where money is constantly spent on gambling at the expense of basic family needs.

1965

Abolition of the death penalty for murder. This is not a simple issue to understand because the death penalty can be used within a nation which is righteous in all its ways. Righteous judgements concerning life and death require the authority which only God can give and which, therefore, must come from the heart of a nation seeking God in all its ways. The removal of this penalty in Britain is a clear indication of how far we have drifted from righteousness in other ways. Those who stand as judge and executioner in relation to murder are to be God's agents for justice. The effect of the death penalty in a righteous nation is that it acts as a deterrent to murder, more than it is a punishment. Though the removal of the death penalty is a removal of one of the most important aspects of the laws of God, it cannot be restored safely in an unrighteous nation, yet while there is no death penalty the deterrent against murder is weakened. In an unrighteous nation the value of life becomes debased and the removal of the death penalty will increase this.

1967

The Abortion Act, later amended in 1990. Abortion is now legal. Babies in the womb can be aborted up to twenty-four weeks into the pregnancy. Doctors can act as judge and jury on the life of a child before it is born, and mothers can ask for their child to be put to death – legally.

1967

The Sexual Offences Act. The most terrible acts of indecency and sexual perversion have now become legal.

1968

The Theatre Act. Censorship has been diluted relating to live performances on the stage, opening the way for abominable practices to be displayed publicly.

1969

The Divorce Law. The loosening of restraints on divorce has led the way to a form of lawful adultery and a cheapening of the most sacred marriage vows. The Family Law Bill which will further weaken the institution of marriage aims to bring in 'no fault' divorce initiatives in the near future.

1993

The Sunday Trading Act. The erosion of legal restrictions on Sunday trading opened the way for the Sabbath to be desecrated with the approval of national leadership and without any sense of wrong.

1994

The National Lottery. Covetousness and greed are built into the national law structures with every law which promotes gambling. This results in an unwritten tax on the poor who are the main contributors to this gambling, based on glossy advertising approved by government, which leads impressionable people to think there is a quick route to wealth, rather than focusing on the just rewards of hard work and service. Furthermore, occult means of prediction are encouraged on the television programme where the winning numbers are announced.

Do we think that mankind is able to live a moral and godly life without restraints? The Bible teaches otherwise. People are like sheep who go astray unless they are led by careful, committed, loving, responsible shepherds. The government is gradually rejecting its responsibility to protect the nation through the law structure, and is giving the responsibility to individuals who are unable to carry it. The leaders of the nation, including prominent churchmen, are the shepherds of the nation as a whole. Unless restraints are put into the law system, providing the boundaries of our freedom, then God's standards will disappear. If you take away the law restraining homosexual practices, such practices will increase. If you legalise pornography, pornography will increase. If you make abortion easy, there will be more abortions. If you make divorce easy, divorce will rise. This is because human nature is fallen. There is a natural tendency to do evil and go against God's laws.

We are responsible for our own sins, and parents are responsible for their children's upbringing, but a nation also needs leaders to set standards, to guide and shepherd in a way that helps individuals to choose the best and most godly way.

If each citizen of Britain were taught the foundational truths of the Bible afresh, we might realise how much we are caught up in the decline of unrighteous Britain now. We would realise that the lawmakers have let us down, legalising things that God says are unlawful. We would see clearly what was needed in our family lives, our financial affairs, our education systems, our care of children, our lifestyle. In the end it is each person who is responsible before God for the sins they have committed, but the leaders of the nation have surely much to answer for. It is time for a new breed of leaders to emerge who will actually lead with some moral fibre, recognising the solemnity of the Coronation Oath and returning to the standards of the Bible, rather than pandering to the latest opinion polls.

12

Repentance

> Or do you show contempt for the riches of his kindness, tolerance, and patience, not realising that God's kindness leads you towards repentance? (Romans 2:4).

How can a loving God bring a mighty earthquake and an economic woe? How can we announce judgement and hardship ahead, and yet claim that God loves us?

The answer is that we have hidden ourselves from God by committing sin. We have brought judgement upon ourselves. Though God is always near, we have turned away from him. There comes a time when God will allow us to reap what we have sown, yet even in this we can know that God loves us. His love is immeasurable. He is perfect love. How much more can he do? He sent his Son into the world to pay the price for our sins, nailed to a cruel Roman cross. If he did not love us he would have abandoned us long ago. But he is infinitely patient. He has continued to bless the people of Britain even when we have turned away from him and he continues to send us warnings. The 'Minus to Plus' campaign and the *Jesus is Alive!* postmark are just two of the testimonies to his love and promise of forgiveness through the atoning blood of Jesus. There are many more. He takes no pleasure in punishing us and he grieves over us even as he sends woeful judgements, but the time of woe inevitably comes to call us to repentance. Even his judgements are backed by his loving character and he is constantly calling us to come to him for forgiveness and a fresh start.

The Woe that is coming is for our own good. God will bring us out of the bondage of our sinful ways and expect us to look to him for rebuilding. This is by no means abandonment. There is hope for us, but we must realise what we must do.

The answer is repentance. The prophecy says: 'If you repent and turn from your wicked ways, I will visit your nation, Great Britain, once again, not with judgement, but with revival power, and I will protect you from all the strategy of the enemy.'

Repentance means turning back to God. It is a principle that God always offers to his people. It is like Jesus' story of the prodigal son. A son persuaded his father to give him his inheritance before the father had died. The son then went and squandered the money on loose living. When it was all gone, he found himself destitute and took a job as a hired servant looking after pigs, even eating what the pigs ate. Then he came to his senses and returned home. He had done wrong. He had left his father. But he was repentant and asked for forgiveness. The father forgave him and brought him back into the home, putting on a special celebration in his honour.

This is what is meant by repentance. We too have squandered the blessings that God has given us, resulting in the most terrible sins – sins that we would not expect anyone to forgive. Yet God is offering us forgiveness at this time through the atoning blood of Jesus Christ. God is offering a fresh start to the whole nation of Britain. John Major's 'back to basics' campaign needs to be resurrected and we need to understand that the 'basics' are to be found in the word of God.

Repentance involves *conviction* of sin, the realisation that we have done wrong. It involves *confession* of sin and it involves *faith* in Jesus Christ. When Jesus Christ went to the cross at Calvary, he paid the price for the sins of us all, so that all who repent will be forgiven – but it cost him everything. That horrific and painful death is the cost of the sins of each one of us. Repentance involves the determination not to sin again.

Repentance is an individual activity. All of us must consider what part we have played in the moral decay of Britain. Most will find that they could blame someone else for leading them astray. This will do no good. We must accept responsibility for our own actions. We must be honest before God and pray to him. Those who are truly sorry will discover that they will be forgiven provided they turn to God in repentance and faith.

Repentance itself is a gift from God. As a person begins to be convicted that they have sinned against God and against their fellow men and women, and prays in the name of Jesus, then God helps them to realise what they have done and their faith grows so that the full process of repentance, forgiveness, restoration and healing can take place. This is where the gentleness, patience and love of God are realised.

It is time for each person in Britain to take the first

step in repentance, by considering what we have done to offend God. At the time of God's favour nothing is too vile for him to forgive if the sinner is truly repentant. This is because of the infinite worth of Jesus' sacrifice for us.

It is time for us to look at our family life, the way we bring up our children, the priorities of our lives, our sport, our entertainment, our personal relationships, the way we handle our money, the way we do our daily work, whether we covet or steal, how we look after our bodies and so on. It is time for us to see how we measure up to the commandments of God.

In times past when God blessed this nation with repentance, he led people to churches and raised up ministers of the gospel to preach messages which have led to conviction of sin and repentance. In the Welsh Revival of 1904, there were stories of people being so convicted of the need to be holy that crime just disappeared from certain areas and policemen and lawyers had little work to do to maintain order and administer justice. Policemen formed choirs instead, to sing Christian hymns. These blessings followed in the wake of a national repentance in Wales as the gospel was preached to congregations in the chapels. When God leads a person to repentance through confession of sin then he really does give them a fresh start. He is the living God and fellowship with him is real. He wants to take his position as the head of every home. After the Welsh Revival families would even leave a spare chair at their dining table for 'the unseen guest' who was Jesus Christ. Such was the impact he had on them.

Sins must be confessed individually, but this could lead to a national repentance. By this we mean a new turning towards God through our government and law structure, and through all our institutions.

If educationalists were moved to repentance, school curriculums would be remodelled to establish teaching which honours God. We are dishonouring him at the moment with much of our teaching in science and the humanities. In science it is taught as an established fact that the universe evolved and that man came from apes. There is genuine controversy over evolution, but this does not filter down to our children. We prefer to ignore the Creator of the universe who also created mankind and placed him as his highest treasure. In humanities we teach about the power of man to manage his own affairs without God. This is an offence against the living God who seeks to guide us and have us understand his work and his ways.

Companies and financial institutions need to repent of their exploitation of the poor, particularly among the less developed nations. The simple principle of using fair scales in our financial dealings must return and so must care of the poor rather than exploitation of them. The financial institutions are masters rather than servants, and love of money and covetousness are rife.

Poorer countries are bound by debts they can never repay. If we were to establish the biblical principle of a Jubilee (Leviticus 25:8–17) and cancel those debts, the poorer nations could properly enter the world community. Why shouldn't Britain give a lead here, perhaps in a carefully modified form that could take account of any dishonest motives? The Jubilee principle requires pure motives for its success.

At government level it is time to have the laws that

honour God's word and bring godly restraint to the nation. It is time to repent of relative morality and bring back absolute standards.

In the church it is time to repent of compromise. There is one true God, and his Son Jesus Christ has paid the price for the sins of the world. There is no other way to be saved. It is time to declare an uncompromising gospel message. It is time for the standards of the Christian life to be declared and lived without ambiguity. It is time for the biblical balance of the roles and responsibilities of men and women to be restored.

It is time for some members of the Royal Family to repent of their poor example over recent years. It is time to look again at the Coronation Oath and confess that we have not kept it as we should.

It is time for universities and colleges to look at what they are teaching. Science which once exalted God as Creator and caused us to worship him in awe and reverence now denies his very existence. The arts do not honour God. They build on humanistic thought and establish gods of their own in the thinking of society, while having the power, through media and fashion, to seduce the nation. In sport, we have exalted man and his performances to divine status. Sport and sportsmen rather than God are worshipped in our national arenas every Sunday.

It is time for Britain to repent of the colonial exploitation of the people in the countries that we have ruled. We need to repent of the missed opportunities in witnessing to Muslim nations of the truths of the Christian faith. The rise of Islam in our day is evidence of this. Muslims are being taught that Britain today represents true Christianity. This is simply not true. The British nation as a whole has never shown the Muslims what a true Christian nation is like.

Repentance is the first part of the process of waking up, when we realise that through seduction of Satan and apathy we have drifted into a kind of sinful slumber. We have mentioned how the Great Awakening of the 1700s was a preparation for the great work of the 1800s. Similarly the 1904 Welsh Revival woke us up and prepared us for the First World War. We are at another climax of world history in our day, perhaps the greatest climax of all time, and God is asking us to wake up, come out of false alliances, particularly Europe, and be a witness for him again.

Perhaps the level of national repentance that is required of us this time is even beyond anything experienced in previous generations. There is one other area that must be mentioned. This is in regard to the Jews and the land of Israel. It was while Britain had the mandate to govern Palestine that we had the opportunity to initiate the return of the land of Israel to the Jews. This was initiated in the Balfour Declaration in November 1917. Later Britain was to turn its back on the Jews even though enough had been done so that Israel returned to the land in 1948. Britain was used by God to initiate one of the last great fulfilments of biblical prophecy, one that heralds the imminent return of Jesus. Not only has God raised us up to be a law-abiding nation that he can bless, he has raised us up for his end-time purposes and we have already failed in this important task. This shows how close we should be to understanding the Bible. The teachings of the Bible go very deep and must be deep-rooted in a nation that serves God in these last days of human history.

Surely God is sending us a dramatic financial judgement, accompanied by a physical earthquake, to wake us up, so that we will seek him through repentance and fresh commitment. He is not sending this mighty earthquake for us to repent in regard to our finances alone, but it is also his device for bringing us back to him in all areas of our lives. Surely he wants to re-establish us through our families, through our institutions and through the church, so that we will be witnesses to the truth of the Bible and the working of his Spirit. We can share in the life and work that he has for those who serve him with undivided hearts, even to the end of the age.

We know from the book of Jonah that there are times when God may warn a Gentile nation. In that case the prophet Jonah warned the city of Nineveh that it would be destroyed. It was a large and prominent city of the ancient world which had turned to wicked ways. God only gave the people forty days to repent, and this seemed to Jonah to be impossible, so wicked had they become. Yet the people did repent, and God did not bring the judgement that had been planned. The repentance was led by the King of Nineveh himself. We cannot be sure when God will deal with us in judgement, so it is a matter of great urgency when he offers us an opportunity to repent.

Britain is in a similar situation to Nineveh; our City is being warned of coming judgement, and we may only have a short time before the judgement comes in the form of an earthquake. Yet it may be possible to repent like the people of Nineveh, and God may then decide not to bring the earthquake after all. Just as at Nineveh, our monarch should lead the nation to repentance. She should summon the ministers of the church and the leaders of the government over whom she has authority, and call the nation to a day of repentance. This should be done with all urgency, because there may not be much time before the judgement falls. If we do not, then the words of Jesus will be true of us: 'The men of Nineveh will stand up at the judgment with this generation and condemn it; for they repented at the preaching of Jonah, and now one greater than Jonah is here' (Matthew 12:41).

13

The Gospel of the Kingdom

> For God so loved the world that he gave his one and only Son, that whoever believes in him shall not perish but have eternal life (John 3:16).

Jesus Christ is the Son of God. He was with the Father before the creation of the world and all things were created by him and for him. He has always been in perfect unity with the Father. He came into this world in the form of a man to show us the way to the Father.

When Jesus went to the cross at Calvary he went to pay the price for our sins through that most painful and terrible death. Each one of us sins. We were born with a sinful nature on account of the sin of Adam and Eve which led to separation from God of them and all mankind. Sin affected every part of God's creation, bringing decay and alienation from God. We were without hope until Jesus came. God sent his only Son into the world to teach us the true meaning of the Scriptures and fully reveal the character of God, and also to be the sacrifice for our sins. If he had not come into the world and offered himself as the sacrifice for our sins then we would have had to suffer the penalty for those sins. That penalty is eternal separation from God. Now that the price is paid there is an invitation into the kingdom of heaven. The condition is faith in Jesus, and acceptance of his lordship in our lives, but each of us must make an individual response.

Jesus said,

> Come to me, all you who are weary and burdened, and I will give you rest. Take my yoke upon you and learn from me, for I am gentle and humble in heart, and you will find rest for your souls. For my yoke is easy and my burden is light (Matthew 11:28–30).

The Bible teaches us that faith comes through hearing this wonderful truth. Those who realise that they have sinned and fallen short of the glory of God, and who truly want to repent of their sins, can at any time turn to God in prayer and seek forgiveness through the shed blood of Jesus. His blood was shed for us, and his life was given for us. In turning to God in repentance, faith will also be given as a gift. This is the moment of moving from darkness to light, from death to life. This is the process of salvation being worked in us. Realisation of sin, confession of sin and turning to God through repentance is the beginning, and asking for forgiveness through the sacrifice of Jesus is the means by which God brings us into new life. God takes the first step in calling us to repentance and faith, but we must respond and accept his invitation.

Those who turn in repentance to Jesus realise they have nothing that they can offer as payment for their sins. Only Jesus can pay that price. It is a free gift received by faith. As it says in Romans 6:23, 'For the wages of sin is death, but the gift of God is eternal life in Christ Jesus our Lord.'

The Spirit of God will come and change the heart at this time of new birth, so that we are able to please God. No sin is too great for Jesus to forgive. No person is beyond hope, and God is able to transform us into a new creation so that we can overcome the temptation to sin. This is incredible, but it is true. In fact, it is a necessary condition for entry into the kingdom of heaven. We must become changed people. Our inner character must change and be transformed into the likeness of Jesus. Jesus made it clear that, 'No-one can see the kingdom of God unless he is born again' (John 3:3). This new birth is in God's hands, who brings us to the point of willing submission. It is a gift from God and we are unable to bring it about ourselves. This new birth brings evidence of a new spiritual life where a person's character is transformed to live a life worthy of God.

In the book of Revelation the invitation to salvation is compared with an invitation to drink pure life-giving water: 'Whoever is thirsty, let him come; and whoever wishes, let him take the free gift of the water of life' (Revelation 22:17).

When the Woe comes upon Britain, many people are going to acknowledge that there is a God in heaven and that, before this holy God, they have sinned. Though this shaking will bring financial collapse to the City, many people will become aware they too have sinned. They will wonder why this has come upon them. Also the Holy Spirit of God will bring conviction of sins, particularly when they hear the preaching of Bible truths. Those who read this book must realise that it is because of all the sins of the nation, and not just the financial sins, that the Woe is coming upon us. When they see what we have prophesied coming to pass, they must realise that it is time to turn away from their sins.

There will be many who have had abortions, many who have committed terrible sexual sins, many who have been dishonest in business, many who have misused their wealth, many who have abused and used others, many who have been following false gods and built up idols in their lives, many who have not lived up to God's standards for family and married life, many who have misled others, many who have blasphemed, many who have been lazy. Every sin will be exposed. This could lead to utter helplessness and despair, but the good news is that God has made provision for our sins so that there can be a new life in Jesus. We need only turn to him in faith. We are free to remain with our guilt, not receiving the gift of salvation but dying in our sins, but there is also an invitation to put everything behind us and start again.

God is building a family. It is an ancient family, going back right through Bible history. It consists of people who believe in God's Son Jesus Christ, who are allowing him to build a new life for them on strong foundations, and letting him prepare them for the kingdom of heaven.

Jesus is coming back soon to gather his kingdom together. The book of Revelation gives us some indications of what that kingdom will be like. There will be no more sin, no more sickness, no more pain. God himself will shed light on the new heaven and the new earth where those who are his will live for ever. The trials of this life are short in comparison with the joys of eternal life ahead for all who submit through faith to King Jesus, and who will live in his kingdom. There is hope.

When the woe comes in the form of a mighty earthquake remember these things; take heart, do not give up, but pray without ceasing and see the salvation of your God. The good news is that Jesus is alive! This is the message that echoes throughout history and transforms lives. It is the most important fact of history, and helps us to lift our eyes above the circumstances of this fallen world and to reach out to that kingdom that is not of this world. Remember, whatever your situation, however broken your life may appear to be, he is inviting you to be a partaker of his life and his kingdom. The problems of this life may seem negative, but he can transform all our negatives to positives through the cross of Jesus.

Everyone who calls upon the name of the Lord will be saved (Romans 10:13).

Jesus is Alive! Ministries

Jesus is Alive! Ministries came into being following the 1988 national postmark campaign of the same name. It is a Christian charity whose primary object is the advancement of the Christian faith throughout the world by the proclamation of the truth that *Jesus is Alive!*

The ministry is both prophetic and evangelistic. Among its specific goals are:

(a) Evangelistic campaigns in the UK and throughout the world, including the promotion of the gospel message to the Jewish people.
(b) Ministry to the inmates of prisons and borstals.
(c) Promotion of education according to Christian principles.
(d) Relief of the poor and the sick.

In fulfilling its prophetic role Jesus is Alive! Ministries is committed to making known the prophecies concerning the three Woes, the first being the earthquake in the City.

For the latest news and information, contact Jesus is Alive! Ministries' web site: http://www.gocin.com/jesusisalive

Jesus is Alive! Ministries
PO Box 5301
Southend on Sea
SS1 1TL.

Tel/Fax: 01702 394077

e-mail: JIAMINSUK@aol.com